BLESSED BISHOP
$\mathcal{N}$ICHOLAS $\mathcal{C}$HARNETSKY, C.Ss.R.
AND COMPANIONS

BLESSED BISHOP
NICHOLAS CHARNETSKY, C.SS.R.
AND COMPANIONS

MODERN MARTYRS OF THE
UKRAINIAN CATHOLIC CHURCH

EDITED BY JOHN SIANCHUK, C.SS.R.

Liguori
LIGUORI, MISSOURI

Published by the Yorkton Province Redemptorists, 250 Jefferson Avenue, Winnipeg, Manitoba, R2V 0M6, (204) 339–5737, and produced by Liguori Publications, Liguori, MO 63057.
http://www.liguori.org
http://www.yorktonredemptorists.com

ISBN 0-7648-0867-2

Library of Congress Catalog Card Number: 2002106826

Printed in the United States of America
06 05 04 03 02   5 4 3 2 3 1
First edition

Pencil Sketch of Blessed Ivan, Blessed Basil, Blessed Nicholas, and Blessed Zenon

Image by Jeannette Shewchuk

CONTENTS

$\mathcal{I}$NTRODUCTION

⁂

O n June 27, 2001, Pope John Paul II beatified twenty-seven martyrs of the Ukrainian Catholic Church during his visit to the city of Lviv, Ukraine. Twenty-five of these martyrs are listed in the Church calendar under the title "Mykolay Charnetsky and Twenty-four Companions." Included with Mykolay (Nicholas) Charnetsky, C.Ss.R., are three other Redemptorists: Bishop Vasyl (Basil) Vsevolod Velychkovsky, Father Ivan Ziatyk, and Father Zynoviy (Zenon) Kovalyk. These Servants of God were officially invoked as "blesseds" on the feast day of Our Mother of Perpetual Help, an icon and a title close to the hearts of all Redemptorists, but especially significant to those Ukrainian Redemptorists whose efforts were placed under her care.

The scope of this book is to present in greater detail the faith-filled stories of these four modern Redemptorist martyrs and the rest of their companions, all of whom died of sufferings and torture inflicted either during World War II or after it, during the era of Soviet control prior to Ukrainian independence in 1991. These Redemptorists and their companions represent a glorious era of martyrdom for the Ukrainian Catholic Church, and their stories give great witness to the strength of their Catholic faith.

First: a brief word about the history of the Ukrainian Catholic Church. Catholic Christianity in its Byzantine-Slavic rite (and linked to the Patriarchate of Constantinople) was introduced to

Ukraine in 988 A.D. At that point in time, no schism had yet caused a division between Eastern and Western Catholic churches. In 1054, when the schism did occur, the effects of this event were not felt in Ukraine for several centuries. In 1596, the Ukrainian Catholic Church reaffirmed its full union with the Holy See in Rome through the Union of Brest. Conflict almost immediately arose as some Ukrainians wished to remain within the Orthodox Church. In 1623, Bishop Josaphat Kunsevych was martyred in the cause of preserving the Union. After the partition of Poland in 1795, Ukraine was divided between Russia and Austria. In the area under Russia (Greater Ukraine), Ukrainian Catholics were forced to become Orthodox. The area under Austria (Western Ukraine) remained predominantly Catholic but still adhering to the Byzantine liturgical and spiritual traditions.

The first Redemptorists, led by Belgian Fathers Joseph Schrijvers and Hector Kinzinger, arrived in Ukraine on November 13, 1913, only at the start of the twentieth century. They came at the invitation of the Archbishop Metropolitan of Lviv. Within a short time, the Redemptorist missionaries who had adopted the Byzantine rite were engaged in the work of parish missions and preserving the fervor of Catholicism in Western Ukraine.

After World War II, Western Ukraine fell under the Communists who immediately began a systematic persecution of the Ukrainian Catholic Church. On April 11, 1945, the entire Ukrainian Catholic hierarchy was arrested, along with many priests and lay Catholics. This Communist persecution lasted until 1988–1989. In 1991, Ukraine finally regained its independence, and the Ukrainian Catholic Church was once again allowed to openly flourish.

The story of these four modern Redemptorist martyrs are told in the following chapters of this book. Brief biographies of their companion martyrs may be found in Appendix 1. We invite you to read and reflect on the stories of these glorious Ukrainian martyrs.

✗ the east was under Commies too.

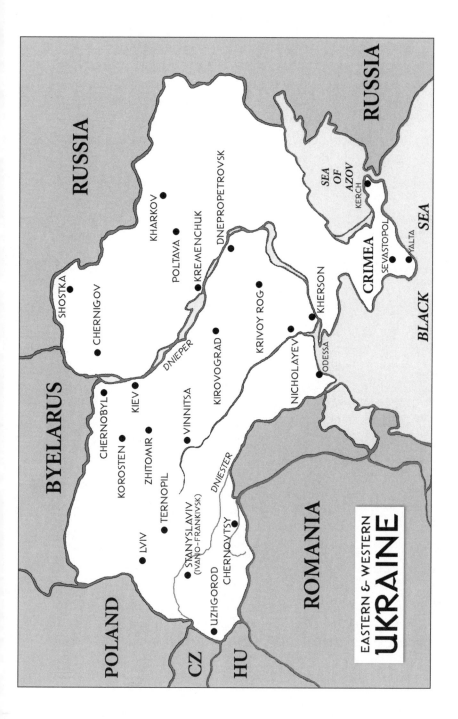

EASTERN & WESTERN
UKRAINE

BLESSED BISHOP
NICHOLAS CHARNETSKY, C.Ss.R.
AND COMPANIONS

Chapter 1

*M*YKOLAY (NICHOLAS) CHARNETSKY, C.SS.R.
1884–1959

The ancient and beautiful Lychakiv cemetery in Lviv holds the grave of Bishop Mykolay (Nicholas in English) Charnetsky. There a steady stream of people from all over Ukraine come to visit the tomb of the martyred bishop, symbol of the survival of Ukrainian Catholicism throughout years of persecution.

Bishop Nicholas's grave site.

NICHOLAS'S BIRTH

Bishop Nicholas was born December 4, 1884, in the western part of Ukraine in the village of Semakivci, a few miles south of the Dniester River near the town of Horodenka. Nicholas, son of Oleksa Charnetsky and Paraska Prytocky, was the first of nine children. He was born into a poor family at a time when many Ukrainians from that district were immigrating to North and South America in search of a brighter future.

Nicholas's birthplace. A chapel now stands on the spot.

Nicholas's mother was orphaned at the age of three by a cholera epidemic that swept throughout Western Ukraine. She was adopted by the family of the pastor of the Ascension of Christ Church in Semakivci. This orphaned child grew up and lived in the parish house until she married Oleska Charnetsky. Since Oleska was poor, the pastor's family helped the young Charnetskys to find a house and some land on which to begin their married life.

The house where Nicholas was born was close to the church. It was clay-daubed with a thatched roof. The dwelling consisted of a single room and a place for hay. Later the Charnetskys sold this house and bought a bigger house with two rooms.

Paraska was a hard worker and she was often called on to help at the parish house. She brought her children to work with her, and thus young Nicholas grew up close to the Church. His mother's adoptive parents were very interested in the welfare of Nicholas who proved himself to be an inquisitive and studious lad.

Cathedral in Stanyslaviv near school attended by Nicholas.

NICHOLAS'S SCHOOLING

Because the school in Semakivci was limited, the pastor's wife arranged to have Nicholas enrolled in the school in Tovmach, whose curriculum would allow Nicholas to become eligible to enter a gymnasium or high school. After finishing school in Tovmach, Nicholas went to Stanyslaviv (now Ivano-Frankivsk) for high school from 1896 to 1904. Then Nicholas had the good fortune to attend the St. Nicholas Bursa, or residence. Besides assuring a good atmosphere for study, living at the Bursa also provided spiritual formation, along with morning and evening prayers. The school was near the cathedral, and so Nicholas would often frequent the cathedral for morning Divine Liturgy (celebration of the Eucharist). The language of instruction at St. Nicholas was Polish, but Ukrainian students attended several classes a week taught in Ukrainian and touching on Ukrainian language, literature, and culture. Thus, this school became a place to foster consciousness of students' Ukrainian heritage.

Nicholas was well respected by his fellow students. A companion of his at the Bursa writes this about him:

Bishop Charnetsky exhibited exemplary conduct; he got along with everyone, and made difficulties for no one. He was inclined to be quiet, meticulous in carrying out his duties, punctual, humble and truthful, envious of no one. In his presence it was not possible to speak evil of anyone, even in jest, or to call anyone names, because he would come to their defense....He wore simple clothes, and was content with what he had. Above all, he was characterized by his piety: he prayed much, and often went to confession and to Holy Communion....I never saw him in an angry mood; he was always gentle in his words and behavior. So it was no wonder that we, his companions, respected him and loved him....

These characteristics stayed with Bishop Nicholas throughout his life, and grew to heroic proportions, especially during his time in the prison camps.

STUDY FOR THE PRIESTHOOD

In 1904, Nicholas applied for enrollment in theology. The bishop of Stanyslaviv, Gregory Khomyshyn, accepted him and sent him for studies to Rome. This is the same bishop who will ordain Nicholas to the priesthood, and later to the episcopacy, who will share in a martyr's death, and who is now listed among the companions of Bishop Nicholas.

Nicholas arrived in Rome in the autumn of 1904 in order to study philosophy and theology. The Ukrainian College in Rome was located on the Piazza Madonna dei Monti, situated between the Quirinale and the Coliseum. The college is only a five-minute walk from the church where Nicholas would later be consecrated a bishop. The students of the Ukrainian College also attended lectures at the *De Propaganda Fide* University along with students of many other nationalities and countries.

Charnetsky studied in Rome for six years—two years of philosophy and four years of theology. He also profited from additional lectures on the thought of Saint Thomas of Aquinas. He made profitable use of his stay in Rome: not only did he attend to his studies diligently but he also tried to learn foreign languages and to understand better the ancient and contemporary Roman and Christian culture.

Nicholas's six-year stay in the Eternal City was an excellent preparation for his future work. He returned to Ukraine a man of great education, of deep piety, and of fiery zeal for apostolic work.

Ukrainian Catholic Major Seminary where Nicholas taught.

ORDINATION TO THE PRIESTHOOD

On October 2, 1909, Bishop Gregory Khomyshyn ordained Nicholas to the priesthood in Stanyslaviv. As a new priest, Father Nicholas celebrated his First Divine Liturgy in his family village of Semakivci. An eyewitness relates that all those present cried with emotion upon seeing a son of their village become a priest. In a special way, this was a day of joy for his parents, seeing their son at the altar, receiving his blessing as he placed his hands on their heads.

After his ordination, Father Charnetsky returned to Rome in order to obtain a doctoral degree in Sacred Theology. With this degree in hand, Nicholas returned to Stanyslaviv in the autumn of 1910 and became professor of philosophy and fundamental dogmatic theology.

As a teacher at the seminary, Nicholas possessed a thorough knowledge of his subjects and an ability to transmit these subjects to students in an accessible way. He was also the spiritual director of the seminarians.

At first Father Charnetsky had two rooms assigned to him at the seminary; but, in order to be close to the students, he moved to a single room. His room was simple and ordinary, his clothing was also simple. Thus, he was very approachable to the students. As a spiritual director, he soon won the love and trust of everyone with his gentleness, love, and humility. Nicholas was always ready to serve others.

The spiritual formation of the seminarians was of deep concern to Nicholas. He did everything to give them a solid basis for that holiness of life that should characterize every priest. He gave an ascetical conference every week; this was characterized by clarity of presentation and flowed from deep conviction. His personal devoutness and holiness spoke louder than the points of meditation he gave every night.

To help the students with their meditation he prepared leaflets which gave suggestions for meditation and particular examination of conscience. To encourage them to develop an intimacy with Christ, he organized the Apostleship of Prayer for the seminarians.

Father Nicholas was also involved with apostolic activity outside the seminary. During his vacations he would visit the elderly. He sought out the sick and would visit them. He had a heart for the poor, the abandoned, the needy.

During World War I, the battlefront went through Stanyslaviv and caused the seminary to close. Many priests had left their posts. Some were conscripted to serve as army chaplains. Many others were arrested, some by the Austrians and others by the Russians. The result was that many parishes in the villages were left without pastoral care. Father Charnetsky began to visit these parishes—usually on foot—in order to offer spiritual care. Because of the unsanitary situations caused by conditions so close to the battlefield, epidemic diseases began to spread. Father Charnetsky, paying no heed to the danger of infection, visited the sick and celebrated the Divine Liturgy in the villages. Ultimately, he became seriously sick with typhus, but he survived. When the fighting moved further east, the seminary reopened and Father Charnetsky resumed his work as a professor and spiritual director with his typical zeal.

JOINING THE REDEMPTORISTS

At the beginning of 1918, two Belgian Redemptorists, Father Joseph Schrijvers and Father Joseph Bala, came to visit the seminary at Stanyslaviv to speak with the students about the Redemptorist Congregation. The Redemptorists had arrived in Ukraine in 1913 and were giving missions to the Ukrainian Catholics as they were already doing for the Ukrainians in Canada. These Redemptorists had accepted the Ukrainian Rite and learned the language. Father Charnetsky recognized through the talks given by these Redemptorists to the seminarians that this congregation stood at a high level of spiritual and apostolic life. He also realized the importance of this Congregation for the Ukrainian people, and so he became its great friend and supporter.

The consequence of this visit was that some of the seminarians decided to enter the Redemptorist congregation. Father Charnetsky, as their spiritual director, assisted them in realizing their decision. Although there was a shortage of priests in the eparchy (diocese) of Stanyslaviv, through the assistance of Father Charnetsky, Bishop Khomyshyn gave his blessing. As a result, two priests entered the Redemptorist Congregation in 1918, and later four seminarians from Stanyslaviv joined also. Finally, Father Charnetsky himself left his post as professor in the seminary and joined the Redemptorists. By choosing to enter religious life in a little-known order, one that was poor and one that was just beginning its work in Ukraine, Father Charnetsky makes a humble choice—one very appropriate to the purpose of the Redemptorists. This was the congregation dedicated to following Jesus Christ the Crucified, to preaching missions to the most abandoned, and to self-abnegation extending even to the love of the cross. And this was precisely what the magnanimous heart of Father Nicholas desired.

In August 1919, Father Charnetsky came to Univ to begin his novitiate under the novice master, Father Hector Kinzinger.

Univ was only a temporary residence; in September 1919, the Redemptorists moved to Zboisk, a village just north of Lviv, which is the capital of Western Ukraine. The property in Zboisk was donated by the Metropolitan to the Redemptorists for the purpose of setting up a religious house there. The residence on the property was not designed to be a monastery, and its one large first-floor room was partitioned with drapes so that there were two rows of small cubicles for the novices. The monastery was very impoverished, not only in furnishings but also in food. The diet was often very simple—bread and potatoes.

On October 15, 1919, Father Nicholas received his Redemptorist habit. Although he had already been a priest for ten years, a professor of philosophy and theology, and a spiritual director for seminarians, he now accepted the role of novice meticulously, readily carrying out all the duties, exercises, and tasks of the novitiate. He was like all the other novices, except for his greater zeal and humility. He was a brother to all the other novices, most of them ten years his junior. During the building of the chapel on their property, Father Nicholas was there, searching for sound usable bricks that were scattered throughout the property, half hidden in the soil. Just over one year later, on October 16, 1920, Father Charnetsky made his religious profession as a Redemptorist.

Father Charnetsky's first assignment after his profession was at the monastery of the Redemptorists in Stanyslaviv. The Redemptorists had been invited there by Bishop Khomyshyn, who gave them a temporary church while they built their own. Father Charnetsky worked very successfully here. While in Stanyslaviv, he also went weekly to the seminary to give spiritual talks. These conferences, permeated by the love of God and given in an engaging way, made a great impression on the seminarians, all the more so because they recognized, from the conversation and the conduct of Father Nicholas that this was a person who lived a holy life. Father Nicholas had such a special talent for integrating into his talks various accounts taken from con-

Nicholas's first assignment at the parish of St. Joseph's in Stanyslaviv.

temporary life that the seminarians eagerly anticipated his wonderful weekly conferences.

The Redemptorists built a large minor seminary in Zboisk, which opened in 1922. Father Charnetsky was called to be one of the instructors for gymnasium-level subjects, even though he was perhaps better suited to teaching theology. Father Charnetsky accepted this position with great humility. In addition, he was also assistant director of novices. During that time, Father Nicholas assisted in preaching many missions, traveling with Redemptorists throughout the towns and villages of Western Ukraine. In 1924, a new Redemptorist house was built in Holosko, which

Redemptorist Major Seminary in Holosko.

was quite close to Zboisk. The clerical novitiate was then transferred here. Father Nicholas spent his time between the two places, giving spiritual conferences to the religious brothers at Zboisk and the clerical novices at Holosko and teaching the students at the minor seminary in Zboisk. Among the novices at Zboisk was Father Vasyl (Basil) Vsevolod Velychkovsky who would later become a bishop, suffer arrest and torture for the faith in prison and concentration camps, and is among the list of companions who were beatified with Bishop Charnetsky.

Despite his numerous occupations Father Charnetsky did not neglect one other aspect of apostolic work—the apostolate of the pen. Following the example of Redemptorist founder, Saint Alphonsus Liguori, who was an extraordinarily prolific theological and spiritual writer, Father Nicholas also occupied himself with literary activity; above all, he tried to put in the hands of people the most popular works of Saint Alphonsus, translating into Ukrainian versions the *Visits to the Blessed Sacrament, The Glories of Mary: Meditations on Mary Most Pure, The Way of the Cross, Meditations on the Most Holy Eucharist,* and *Short Medi-*

tations on the Passion of Jesus Christ for Every Day of the Week. All these were incorporated into a prayer book published at Zhovkva in 1923, with a second edition being published in 1930. This period of Father Nicholas's life ended in 1926 when Nicholas returned home for his father Oleksa's funeral and he received a new assignment.

A NEW MISSION FOR CHURCH UNITY

On April 3, 1926, Father Joseph Schrijvers, the superior of the Redemptorists, sent Father Nicholas Charnetsky to work for the re-union of the Church in Volyn. This was a new field of apostolic work for the Redemptorists. Volyn is that part of Ukraine just north of Halychyna. After the various partitions of Poland in 1772, 1792, and 1795, the area of Volyn found itself under the Russian Empire, while Halychyna, even though close by, became part of the Austro-Hungarian Empire. In Volyn, where the Ukrainian Catholic Church had existed before the partitions of Poland, the Russian Empire forcibly suppressed the Ukrainian Catholic Church and replaced it with the Russian Orthodox Church. Even though most of this suppression took place in the early 1800s, some areas of Volyn did not become Orthodox until as late as 1885. With the end of World War I, however, Volyn and Halychyna again became Polish territory.

After World War I, many Ukrainian Catholics from Halychyna chose to settle in the northwestern parts of Ukraine, locating in Volyn because it still had much open land for acquisition. These Ukrainian Catholics who settled in Volyn were without any Ukrainian Catholic priests and therefore were without spiritual care. They did not feel at home in the local Polish Roman Catholic churches, nor did they want to join the Russian Orthodox Church. Because of this they had a need for Ukrainian Catholic priests to serve them.

At the same time, local Orthodox Ukrainians who had once been Ukrainian Catholics before the partitions of Poland persistently sent delegations to Metropolitan Andrew Sheptytsky and to other Ukrainian bishops asking them to send Ukrainian Catholic priests to Volyn. On March 23, 1923, a Peremyshl delegation of Volyn peasants came to Bishop Josaphat Kotsylovsky and requested a Ukrainian Catholic priest to serve their church. The members of the delegation told how they gathered together in church every Sunday and sang the services under the direction of their psalmist-cantor, utilizing, for their services, liturgical books from the time of the Union of Brest; they were aware that their grandfathers had lived in union with the Rome.

Finally, on March 28, 1926, the Latin-Rite bishop of Lutsk, Adolph Szelazek, invited the Redemptorists of the Eastern Rite to help him in the work of the re-union of the shattered strands of the Church in Volyn, uniting those who had remained Orthodox in liturgy and church laws, but who were inclined to acknowledge the pope as their head. Father Nicholas was sent by his superior in response to this request. Father Nicholas now begins an apostolic work that will consume him, a work that became very close to his heart. He will for the next fourteen years be involved with the work and the struggles of Church unity.

The first task of Father Nicholas was to prepare four priests and a deacon for re-union with the Catholic Church. These men had indicated a desire to be received back into the Ukrainian Catholic Church. As a professor, Father Charnetsky was able to instruct and prepare them well. Using the Orthodox liturgical books and sources of these men, he was able to reconcile for them the theological controversies that had kept the Orthodox and Catholic Churches apart. Unfortunately, lured by money, some of these "newly converted" priests returned to the Orthodox Church.

To gain a better understanding of the religious conditions in Volyn, Father Charnetsky undertook two excursions through the country. During these trips, he frequently celebrated the Divine Liturgy and preached primarily for the Ukrainian Catholic settlers from Halychyna who lived scattered throughout all of

Volyn. Many Orthodox also came to these services, often several hundred. They came sometimes with their choir and sang the Liturgy. Father Charnetsky recognized the sympathy of the Orthodox toward re-union; they desired only that they might retain their rites.

After his two excursions through Volyn, Father Charnetsky prepared a report and sent it to the Vatican office concerned with the Eastern Churches, called the Congregation of the Oriental Churches, and also to his superior; in this report, he outlined the possibilities of Church re-union in Volyn. This letter made a great impression everywhere, especially on Cardinal L. Sincero, the Vatican Secretary in charge of issues relating to the Eastern Churches. As a result, he became greatly interested in the problem of Church re-union.

For a place of residence, the Redemptorists, with the permission of Bishop Szelazek, chose Kostopil, a little town in the Volynian part of Polisia. On October 22, 1926, Father Gregory Shyshkovych and Nicholas Charnetsky moved into the house together with two religious brothers. Shyshkovych was the superior. The dwelling was small with paper-thin walls. It was not at all conducive to any sense of recollection, for it was right on the street next to a carpentry shop. However, the room which served for a chapel was always overfilled. The services were done in the full Orthodox fashion, fully sung. The daily Divine Liturgies lasted at least an hour and a quarter, while the Sunday liturgies were much longer. Some two hundred fifty people crowded the little chapel.

Once the Ukrainian Catholics learned that there were Ukrainian Catholic priests in their district, they would travel great distances to come to Divine Liturgy and to receive the sacrament of penance. Often the people had not received the sacraments for many years.

The religious house in Kostopil was a center to which not only the Ukrainian Catholics turned but also many Orthodox who desired to come to re-union with the Ukrainian Catholic

Church. The Redemptorists were becoming known for their apostolic zeal, their great preaching, their genuine concern for the spiritual health of the people. There was a desire among many of the Orthodox to reunite; however much uncertainty also existed about the future of the Redemptorist mission. A great need was felt for a measure of stability. A Ukrainian Catholic parish had to be established, meaning that the Redemptorists, a congregation dedicated to mission work, would have to take on the responsibilities of pastors for these people.

The establishment of a parish was not just a simple task. Since the Redemptorists were outside the jurisdiction of the Metropolitan Archbishop of Lviv and since there was no Ukrainian Catholic Bishop in Volyn, they fell under the Latin-Rite Ordinary. Often, the Latin-Rite bishop had a different agenda than the Eastern-Rite Redemptorists.

Opposition to Re-Union

On January 4, 1927, Father Charnetsky visited the Latin bishop of Lutsk to request permission for the Fathers to maintain the parish. The bishop categorically denied their request, and ordered that all Ukrainian Catholics and those newly reunited with the Catholic Church must be subject in everything to the Latin-Rite pastor at Kostopil. This development placed the Redemptorists in a very delicate position. They were sure that the Ukrainian Catholics would not accept this situation because of their fear of becoming Latinized and even Polonized. This fear was well-grounded since religion had often been used as a cloak for political gain. Orthodox adherents would most certainly be suspicious that the Redemptorists were agents of Polonization as well. On the other hand, the Latin-Rite bishops and, perhaps more so, the government was afraid that the Redemptorists would be agents of Ukrainianization. Thus, a non-Ukrainian, Father Richard Costenoble, a Redemptorist from Belgium, was placed in charge of the mission. The situation had became extremely tenuous; and there existed a temptation to abandon this new apostolic work. However, Father Charnetsky remained firm in working for re-union despite all these obstacles.

The Redemptorists working in Volyn were the target of opposition from both the Latin-Rite Catholic Church and from the Russian Orthodox Church. Thus, it was necessary to have a deep faith and strong hope that Divine Providence would arrange for this situation to change for the better. It was necessary to hope against hope.

INTENSE APOSTOLIC ACTIVITY

Father Charnetsky, full of optimism and trust in God, continued to persevere and to work zealously. By his spirit and example, he encouraged those who worked with him. All of them saw the great need in Volyn for apostolic work, both for the settlers from Halychyna as well as for the Orthodox who sincerely desired to return to union with the Ukrainian Catholic Church.

Meeting the needs of the settlers from Halychyna and the desires of the Orthodox who wanted re-union with the Ukrainian Catholic Church, Father Nicholas and his confreres developed out of Kostopil a very intensive apostolic activity, going out of their monastery to the various areas of Volyn. People flocked to them in large numbers, both settlers from Halychyna as well as the Orthodox; they listened to their sermons attentively and warmly invited them into their communities. This favorable view of the Orthodox toward the Ukrainian Catholic Church was not a passing fancy, but flowed from a deep conviction, as is shown by the number of parishes which accepted re-union.

The inhabitants of the village of Dubechno applied to the bishop for a Ukrainian Catholic priest. On April 21, 1927, the bishop of Lutsk asked the Redemptorists to send a priest to this village. Father Shyshkovich was sent. He had great success in bringing the Word of God and the sacraments to them. Some three thousand signed up for the newly created parish in Dubechno. A diocesan priest, Father Grosh, was assigned as the permanent parish priest of this place.

Father Charnetsky was assigned to another village asking for re-union. On May 15, 1927, Father Nicholas went to Kraska. Through his work among them, all but two families from the entire village accepted re-union. This parish, too, was placed under the pastorship of Father Grosh. The whole village became spiritually alive after this event. Three other villages soon followed. More villages would have followed soon but, unfortunately, no Ukrainian Catholic priests were available to be their pastors.

The religious house in Kostopil was not really the most appropriate center for re-union activities. It proved necessary to choose some town that was bigger and more suitable. As a result, the Redemptorist Fathers moved to Kovel, further north and west of Kostopil. This was the capitol of the region and also a railway center. On September 11, 1927, the Redemptorists— Father Richard Costenoble, Father Gregory Shyshkovych, Father Nicholas Charnetsky, and Brothers Avksenty and Ephrem— moved into a rented house and began their ministry in Kovel where the Orthodox began by the hundreds to visit the temporary chapel of the Fathers. In Kovel, the Fathers opened up very intensive apostolic activity. The animator of their work was Father Charnetsky. Everyone was attracted by his goodness, his gentleness, in conjunction with the spirit of mortification and penance so characteristic of the ascetics of the Eastern Church. Here, too, they served primarily the settlers from Halychyna many of whom had not seen their own priests for several years. They received Father Nicholas with tears; and then the big work began: confessions, marriages, the establishment of a cemetery, the building of a chapel—work which would continue into the following years.

The Redemptorists often traveled many miles to reach the colonies where Ukrainian Catholics lived. Many Orthodox also returned to the union with the Ukrainian Catholic Church through their efforts. To the monastery in Kovel came people who wanted to learn the teachings of the Catholic Church; among them were Orthodox priests and professionals. The Redemptorist Fathers began to give regular catechetical instructions.

In the fall of 1928, Father Shyshkovych was transferred to Canada to assist the Redemptorists who were working among the Ukrainian Catholics there. In his place Father Vasyl (Basil) Vsevolod Velychkovsky came to Kovel. He proved to be a powerful preacher and did much to further the cause of re-union.

This work of re-union generated much opposition. On the one hand, the Russian Orthodox Church opposed it, for they were losing parishioners and congregations. On the other hand, the Polish authorities did not favor a Ukrainian Catholic presence in that territory since it might foster a trend toward independence.

Soon it was apparent that the Ukrainian Catholics of Volyn needed their own bishop. This appointment would secure their canonical existence and would give confidence to those who were re-uniting with the Ukrainian Catholic Church. As would be expected, the Polish government opposed the plan to appoint a bishop for Volyn.

In fact, opposition to the Redemptorists re-union efforts was so great from both the Latin-Rite Polish Catholic Church and the Russian Orthodox factions that the Redemptorist superior was going to withdraw from this ministry. This action could be seen as disappointing, since a Redemptorist departure would leave the settlers from Halychyna spiritually abandoned and in danger of losing their faith. However, at that very same time, new impetus came from Rome in favor of the work of re-union, and thus, with new hope, the Redemptorists remained and continued their work of building the Ukrainian Catholic Church.

During these years, Father Charnetsky's regular apostolic work in Volyn was interspersed with mission work and with lectures at various seminaries, especially in a newly established semi-

Bishop Nicholas at his consecration as bishop in Rome.

nary in Dubno, set up for training Latin-Rite priests who wished to work in the Eastern-Rite Church. He lectured on the liturgy, on pastoral theology, on the conduct of mission, and other topics. He also gave several retreats to pastors in the region and to the Redemptorist minor seminarians in Zboisk.

BECOMING A BISHOP

The apostolic work in Volyn necessarily demanded the establishment of an Eastern-Rite eparchy, or diocese, for these territories. This idea was set forth at a Church Unity Congress in

Pinsk in April 1930. Though the Poles opposed such an idea, a compromise was reached, and Rome named Father Nicholas Charnetsky, C.Ss.R., titular bishop of Lebedos on January 16, 1931, appointing him also Apostolic Visitator for the faithful of the Ukrainian Rite beyond Halychyna.

Father Nicholas was very reticent about this honor: "I have been struck by thunder," he wrote to a friend. One of the Fathers who lived with him also wrote about his response: "When Father Nicholas received the nomination for bishop, he went to Rome, and there represented himself as absolutely unsuitable and unworthy to be a bishop. However, after discussion with the Superior General of the Redemptorists and with the Pope, he was marvelously transformed: though still very unassuming, he nevertheless became conscious that God demanded of him this sacrifice—the elevation to the episcopacy—and showed himself determined and ready for any sacrifice and work that God would ask of him; he appeared full of Divine strength."

Father Charnetsky's episcopal consecration took place on Sunday, February 8, 1931, in the Redemptorist church attached to the Mother House in Rome before the miraculous icon of the Mother of Perpetual Help. The bishop who ordained him, Bishop Gregory Khomyshyn of Stanyslaviv, was also the principal consecrator. The entire service was celebrated with all the magnificence of the Eastern Rite and was sung by the choir of the Ukrainian College—a choir to which Bishop Nicholas belonged when he studied in Rome.

During the ceremony something unusual and rather embarrassing happened. The *mitra*, or bishop's crown, which Bishop Khomyshyn had placed on the head of the newly consecrated Bishop Nicholas fell to the foot of the altar. Involuntarily, those present took this as a bad sign. To those who were near him, Bishop Charnetsky made the following comment: "It will fall again, but then it will be together with my head, as it happened with Saint Josaphat." Bishop Nicholas's life, of course, would eventually be crowned with a martyr's death, although as a result of persecution and imprisonment rather than actual bloodshed.

During the celebrations following Bishop Nicolas's consecration, some rather interesting remarks were made. At the Redemptorist gathering after the official celebrations, Father General Patrick Murray said: "Without doubt our newly consecrated bishop will encounter numerous and great difficulties and obstacles of every sort, perhaps even martyrdom itself."

Bishop Nicholas also spoke, reflecting on the role of the Redemptorists in Ukraine. He explored the reasons why, of all the religious institutes, God had chosen the family of Saint Alphonsus to accomplish an apostolate quite innovative in the Church—namely, the transplanting of a Latin religious order into an Eastern Rite. He observed that the spirit of the Congregation of the Most Holy Redeemer—because of its simplicity, love of sacrifice and self-denial, and also because of its singular devotion to the suffering and eucharistic Jesus and to the Most Holy Virgin Mother of God—was very close to the spirit of the Ukrainian people, and created, as it were, a link of mystical affinity. Thus, it was no wonder that Ukrainians highly valued the work of the Redemptorists and that this work had borne such bountiful fruits.

BACK IN VOLYN

Very soon, difficulties began for the new bishop. The Polish government was unwilling to acknowledge him, the minister of religious affairs in Warsaw not even deigning to receive Bishop Nicholas in an audience. He alleged that "I know the priest Charnetsky, but I don't know any bishop by that name." In spite of this snub, the bishop went on to Volyn and took up residence in the Redemptorist monastery in Kovel.

Soon after his arrival, the house in which the Redemptorists lived became canonically confirmed as a monastery. Also a large, wooden church, called the *Piechotnaia* church, was released to the Redemptorists for the care of Ukrainian Catholics. This church could hold two thousand persons. A new brick monastery was then built on the vacant property behind the church.

After his return from Rome, Bishop Nicholas immediately set about fulfilling his pastoral duties. In three months, he visited forty villages and towns, presiding at devotional services and Divine Liturgies. On these occasions, he zealously proclaimed the Word of God, exhorting all to unity of faith with the center of true orthodox Christianity—Rome. The number of Ukrainian Catholics in Volyn increased constantly but, unfortunately, Bishop Nicholas did not have enough priests to meet the needs of the many parishes that desired to re-unite with the Apostolic See. However, as the desire for Church unity increased among the Orthodox, three Orthodox priests accepted re-union with the Ukrainian Catholic Church.

By 1933, fifty-six villages asked to be accepted back into the Ukrainian Catholic Church. They had to be refused because they lacked priests of their own, while priests from Halychyna were not allowed to come to their assistance. As well, in 1934, thirty villages in Volyn sent signed petitions asking to be received into re-union. Unfortunately, the answer was identical to the requests of 1933.

Because of the shortage of priests, Bishop Szelazek had organized a seminary of the Eastern Rite in Dubno back in 1928. However, this seminary had not prospered, and had, from June 1929 to the summer of 1931, been inactive. After the canonical visitations which Bishop Charnetsky made in 1931 and his subsequent report to Rome, Pope Pius XI decided to reactivate this seminary, placing it under the direction of Jesuit Fathers who were of the Eastern Rite. Bishop Nicholas was one of the professors, commuting from Kovel for his lectures. This seminary helped to provide him with at least some of the much-needed priests for his people.

Bishop Charnetsky himself was very sensitive to the liturgical prescriptions of the Eastern Rite. In Halychyna over the centuries many of the "orthodox" practices had been Latinized through laxity and assimilation. In Volyn, this Latinization had not occurred to any great extent. Those who were Orthodox continued to practice the fullness of the Eastern Rite. Bishop Charnetsky himself practiced the full Orthodox ritual and insisted that the priests who came to serve in Volyn do the same. He was not only sensitive to the external practice of the ritual, but also to Eastern theology with its roots in antiquity.

Bishop Nicholas in 1933.

Bishop Nicholas loved the Eastern Rite and all of its traditions. It was his outstanding concern to observe these traditions with careful exactness. He was mindful of the renowned injunction by Pope Pius X: "No more, no less, no differently" than the Rite prescribes.

This exactness endeared him to the Orthodox people. However, the Orthodox authorities were suspicious and afraid of him. In an article written in an Orthodox journal, warning the faithful against "the false shepherd," he is described in this way: "By his external appearance itself, he (that is, Bishop Nicholas) represents the typical eastern monk [priest], with a big black beard and long hair. And in intellectual matters he exhibits superior culture: he speaks many languages; he has profound knowledge of Ukrainian literature, ancient and modern; and Orthodox theology has no secrets for him. In addition to all this, he possesses admirable tact, great facility of speech, and the ability to discuss and debate exhaustively. While he was still a regular Redemptorist missionary in Volyn in 1925, he knew how to establish ties with many Orthodox priests. In numerous parishes he won over enthusiastic supporters who regarded him as a very devout and learned *batiushka* (meaning 'Little Father,' an affectionate term for an Orthodox priest), different, in their eyes, from other *batiushka* only in this minor detail—that he mentioned the Pope in his Divine Liturgies."

On one occasion, a "separated brother" attempted to drown Bishop Nicholas while he was swimming. Bishop Nicholas's strength overcame his antagonist and he got away from him, though not without losing his shoes. Bishop Nicholas requested that this incident be kept quiet so as not to antagonize the tense situation even more.

Bishop Nicholas's work for re-union was further hampered when the Polish authorities began to confiscate Orthodox church buildings in 1938. More than one hundred forty Orthodox churches were appropriated by the Poles and changed into Roman Catholic *kostels,* or churches; and another one hundred eighty-nine Orthodox church buildings were completely demolished or simply burned down. A protest against this program was raised by Metropolitan Archbishop Andrew Sheptytsky for which the Orthodox were grateful. Bishop Nicholas painfully felt the horror of the Orthodox churches being destroyed by the Polish government, because by this "they frightened [people] away from the Union, and set back the cause of church re-union at least a hundred years."

Under these conditions, the work for church re-union demanded great heroism, self-sacrifice, and exceptional trust in Divine Providence. Bishop Nicholas had such a trust, revitalized in him by a spirit of prayer. For him, his spiritual children were his consolation—the faithful in Volyn who surrounded their bishop with great love and respect. They called him their bishop and considered him as a representative of Metropolitan Archbishop Andrew Sheptytsky, who commanded the highest respect and trust among the Orthodox of Volyn and other territories of Ukraine, even though Bishop Nicholas's appointment came from Rome and even though Metropolitan Sheptytsky had no official authority over this area.

Bishop Charnetsky's people were good and sincere, and all of them were poor: their living conditions were simple with regard to both food and housing. The bishop likewise lived a poor and simple life and paid no attention whatsoever to all the inconveniences that this involved. It seemed that these impoverished circumstances made no impression on him at all. To sleep in a simple village hut, or in the barn, or in some stable on the straw or hay—none of this really bothered him: he accepted whatever was available with the greatest graciousness and with the utmost of understanding. Never did he demand anything special for himself. He was, after all, an apostle of the poor, and himself lived poorly. When he returned home and his colleagues found straw on his clothes and in his pockets and brought this to his attention, he would simply reply, "Well, I didn't want to inconvenience the poor people."

Bishop Nicholas dressed in a simple and plain manner, having the appearance of an ordinary priest. One afternoon in 1939, Bishop Charnetsky, having important business with the rector of the Lviv Seminary, Father Josyf Slipyj, arrived at its door, greeted the porter, and asked to be announced to the Father Rector. The porter, mistaking the bishop for one of the Studite brothers, sharply explained that Father Rector received no one in the afternoon. After a moment's pause, Bishop Charnetsky again spoke to the porter: "I would ask you to announce me to Father Rector, as I have no time to waste." The annoyed porter responded, "You do not seem to understand what I have already told you: Father Rector receives nobody in the afternoon." Then Bishop Nicholas said, "Tell Father Rector that Bishop Charnetsky has arrived." The embarrassed porter fell to his knees and began to apologize; Bishop Nicholas quieted him, remarking "Please continue to do your duties conscientiously, and don't let this bother you; but please do announce me to Father Rector because I really do not have any time to waste." The porter immediately ushered Bishop Charnetsky into the seminary, and ran to summon the Father Rector.

In his apostolic work as a preacher, he was not distinguished by exceptional oratorical talent, but his sermons were always characterized by clarity of expression and by logical organization, and were solidly based on the evangelical truths; most importantly, his listeners were convinced that his teaching flowed from deep personal conviction, and that he himself, in his own life, fully practiced what he preached. He never harangued, never berated, but proffered the Christian teaching of love of God and neighbor, to the extent that the Orthodox said of him, comparing him to their own priests: "Our priests would do better if they preached like that priest, instead of wasting time in attacking him."

Bishop Charnetsky gave himself to prayer, day and night, so that it could be said that his whole life was an unceasing and uninterrupted prayer to God. Never did he pass a day without fulfilling all his spiritual exercises, the Way of the Cross, rosaries,

Charnetsky, Sheptytsky, Ziatyk, and Kovalyk (plus others) on the twenty-fifth anniversary of the Redemptorists in Ukraine.

the *chasoslov* (Divine Office), plus frequent visits to the Blessed Sacrament and to Our Mother of Perpetual Help.

Bishop Nicholas did not limit his apostolic activity to Volyn alone, but as much as possible he hurried with spiritual help anywhere that he might do some good, keeping always and especially in mind the good of the Ukrainian Catholic Church and its development. He also visited other Redemptorist communities in Europe, in Czechoslovakia, Austria, Belgium, and England. Here he would celebrate the Divine Liturgy, giving him the opportunity to teach others about the Eastern Churches and in particular about the Ukrainian Catholic Church.

In his ecumenical activities, Bishop Charnetsky sought to utilize yet another forum, namely the international congresses devoted to church unity. He was actively involved in many such congresses: The Fifth Velehrad Congress in 1927; a Church Unity Conference held in Pinsk in 1931; the Fifth Church Unity Conference also held in Pinsk in 1935; the Seventh Velehrad Congress of 1936; and the Fifth International Congress "For a Christian East" held in 1937. He also organized and chaired a church unity conference in Lviv in 1936.

Bishop Nicholas, a frequent visitor to the Redemptorist seminaries in Kboisk and Holosko, also ordained many of the Redemptorist students. He would travel to Belgium to ordain seminarians there and later traveled to Holosko when the Redemptorist opened their theologate there. Among those ordained by him would be the future Metropolitan of Canada, Maxim Hermaniuk, C.Ss.R., and numerous other Redemptorists.

Throughout his episcopal ministry, the Redemptorists came to help him in Volyn, preaching missions and serving the faithful in ordinary pastoral care. During these missions, Redemptorists would establish confraternities in honor of Our Mother of Perpetual Help. Bishop Nicholas also had a great personal devotion to her. In addition, Bishop Nicholas would participate in events organized by the Redemptorists. He participated in a follow-up to the huge "Youth for Christ" rally in Lviv in 1933

27

and took an active role in the Redemptorist mission organized in Ternopil where he confessed the faithful for many hours at a time.

DURING THE SECOND WORLD WAR

When the Germans attacked Poland on September 1, 1939, Bishop Nicholas was in Lviv. He had come there to ordain some Redemptorists to the priesthood. By September 22, the Soviet army was already in control of Western Ukraine. Bishop Nicholas was prevented by the Soviets from returning to Volyn, and so he remained in the Redemptorist monastery in Lviv. Secretly, he heard confessions and celebrated the Divine Liturgy. On December 22, 1939, together with Metropolitan Andrew Sheptytsky, Bishop Nicholas consecrated Josyf Slipyj as bishop in order to ensure a successor to the Metropolitan See. Bishop Josyf would later be arrested at the same time as Bishop Nicholas and they would spend years in concentration camps together. Eventually, after eighteen years in prison, Bishop Josyf would be released to go to the West and participate in the Second Vatican Council.

During the winter of 1939, Soviet security forces, an arm of the NKVD, moved into the first floor of the monastery where Bishop Nicholas lived. All fifteen Redemptorists were then forced to live in close quarters on the second floor under the continuous eye of the NKVD. A church was attached to the monastery and the Redemptorists continued to serve there. Soon it became a center for religious activity. Bishop Nicholas, since he was stranded in Lviv, spent most of his time in the confessional.

During this time, the cupboards of the monastery were often bare. Friends of the Redemptorists, who were aware of this situation, smuggled in bags of bread, risking dangerous consequences because of the presence of the security police.

In June 1941, the Germans arrived in Lviv and the Soviet Army was forced to retreat. Before leaving the Soviets murder over six thousand prisoners. Among them was Father Zenon Kovalyk, C.Ss.R., also a resident of the Redemptorist monastery who had been arrested in 1940.

[handwritten margin note: why was he arrested only?]

The religious situation became somewhat more favorable under the Germans even though Bishop Charnetsky was still not allowed by the German authorities to return to Volyn. However, the Redemptorists were able to continue their missionary work until 1944 when the Soviet Army returned.

To safeguard the future of the Church and the faithful, on March 13, 1940, Metropolitan Sheptytsky convoked an eparchial synod in Lviv. This synod was in permanent session for four years. Bishop Charnetsky participated in this synod which gave stability to the Church in such uncertain times.

On June 30, 1941, the theological academy in Lviv was reopened and remained open for three years. Bishop Nicholas became one of the professors, and taught philosophy, psychology, and moral theology. One of his former students described the peaceful disposition of the bishop and his complete trust in Divine Providence: "During the bombing of Lviv we were in the study hall. For some time the sirens were signaling that the enemy attack was imminent. The bishop was not bothered by this, and continued his lecture. When the bombs began to explode, the seminarians were completely frightened. The bishop noticed this and, with utter calm, he asked them, 'Would you like to take shelter in the basement? Please, then, do so. We are, however, all of us, in God's hands.'"

During this time, Bishop Nicholas also served the imprisoned and visited those with mental illness at a hospital in Kulpark; and he continued to ordain Redemptorists and other diocesan seminarians.

ARREST OF BISHOP CHARNETSKY

On July 27, 1944, the area of Halychyna again came under Soviet occupation. The death of Metropolitan Andrew Sheptytsky occasioned the beginning of a ruthless persecution of the Ukrainian Catholic Church. On the night between April 10 and April 11, 1945, the entire Ukrainian Catholic episcopate was arrested: Metropolitan Josyf Slipyj and Bishops Gregory Khomyshyn, Ivan Liatyshevsky, Nicetas Budka, and Nicholas Charnetsky.

Monastery where Bishop Nicholas was arrested.

Bishop Nicholas was arrested at the Redemptorist monastery in Lviv on Zyblikevych Avenue, on April 10, 1945, at eight o'clock at night. Six agents of the police, typically robbers and drunkards, arrived at the Redemptorist monastery and demanded to see the superior, Father Joseph De Vocht. When Father De Vocht appeared, the police commandant asked: "Is your name De Vocht? Are you the head of this house? Who else lives here?"

As soon as Father De Vocht mentioned the name "Charnetsky," the commandant exclaimed, "So he *is* here!"

Bishop Charnetsky's room where he lived before he was arrested.

"Yes," replied Father De Vocht, "but he is ill."

"Take me to him!"

The commandant entered the room of the bishop, where all the Redemptorists had gathered for recreation. The commandant immediately forbade anyone to leave the room. As Bishop Nicholas stood up, one of the agents went up to him and searched him to see if he carried any weapon. Several agents then began to search the bishop's room, while two other agents kept an eye on the Redemptorist confreres. An agent discovered a brochure and with a sarcastic smile held it up and sneered, "And priests don't meddle with politics, eh?!" A container of old papers was emptied into a bag. They examined all of the bishop's books very carefully. In one of the drawers of the desk where the bishop worked, they found six hundred rubles—in paper money of little value. They then confiscated some chalices, reliquaries, the bishop's pectoral cross, and his ring. A small sum of money, well tucked away by the bishop, managed to escape their notice.

Then the lengthy interrogation began. When they came across some penitential chains, an agent asked, "And what are

Some artifacts of Bishop Nicholas's kept hidden from the Soviets.

these?" Father De Vocht replied that they were for self-mortification. The agent turned away with disdain.

By this time it was 10:45 at night. An agent found a key in Bishop Charnetsky's room, and the agent demanded to know its use. The bishop replied that this was the key to the library. The bishop had reluctantly bought clothing and other necessities for himself but his great love was books. These he bought from bookstores that sold books confiscated by the Soviets from monastery libraries. The bishop especially strove to buy books in Lviv, since his library in Kovel had been destroyed by fire during the war.

The agent ordered the bishop to take him to this library which was done. Also in the library were two typewriters, as well as the bishop's episcopal vestments and some other clothes.

When they returned to the bishop's room, the commandant informed the bishop that the time had come for Bishop Nicholas to leave. He was allowed to take along a little clothing, a pillow, and one quilt. Dressed in a simple cassock made from cheap material, with his overcoat, and carrying an old pair of boots, the bishop took leave of his confreres, all of whom were overcome by emotion. On the threshold of his room, the bishop turned to Father De Vocht and asked him to give a final absolution. At the door of the monastery waited a covered vehicle, a black police van. The vehicle sped away into the darkness.

This was a very painful parting of the bishop with his confreres; they were never again to see Bishop Nicholas alive. On orders from the commandant, all members of the community had to disperse immediately to their rooms; only one, the youngest, named Mayik, had to remain. Mayik watched while they packed the chalices, the bishop's vestments, and all the rest; then he was forced to sign a statement that read thusly: "On April 11, 1945, at 1:00 A.M., Charnetsky, Nicholas, was arrested by agents of the NKVD [security police], and all was done according to legal prescriptions, and without acts of violence." They then sealed the doors to the bishop's room and the library. After this, all twenty-six agents of the NKVD—twenty agents had been assigned to stand guard outside the monastery—departed.

IMPRISONMENT

Bishop Charnetsky was taken to the Lviv prison. During his stay there, Father De Vocht and other confreres managed to locate where he was being kept in order to send him clothing and food. Later, the bishop was transferred to Kiev as were the rest of the Ukrainian bishops. His Redemptorist confreres also succeeded in learning where the bishop was imprisoned in Kiev, and regularly sent him articles of food and clothing there.

The bishop remained in prison in Kiev for about eighteen months; and here he underwent endless interrogations accompanied by cruel treatment. These interrogations took place at night, as was the custom in Soviet prisons. This type of investigation is unique: its purpose is not to uncover from the prisoner any truth of the matter, but to elicit from the accused a confession of his "crimes," which in truth he or she had not committed. The interrogations take place in conditions that can shatter the nerves, the self-worth, and the morale of the person being targeted. Sometimes drugs are used, even surreptitiously at times, to achieve predetermined ends.

Though we have no specifics about the investigations carried out on Bishop Charnetsky, we do know he underwent about six hundred hours of terrible interrogation during his ten years in prison at the hands of the Soviet secret police. We can only conclude, from the comparison of his appearance before his arrest with his appearance after his return from exile, how great and cruel must have been the treatment that the bishop underwent.

In Kiev, Bishop Nicholas was sentenced, first, to five years of hard labor. Then a witness, an apostate Catholic, alleged that the bishop was "an agent of the Vatican" as the Apostolic Visitator of the Ukrainian Catholics for Volyn. Consequently, his sentence was transmuted to imprisonment in forced-labor camps.

After sentencing, Bishop Nicholas was then incarcerated in a whole series of concentration camps, or gulags, scattered throughout northeastern ASSR (Autonomous Soviet Socialist Republic) of Komi: Mariinsk in the depths of Siberia; the camps of the Pechora River basin, Vorkuta in the far polar north, Inta, and Potma; the transit prison in Kirov northeast of Moscow; and slave-labor camps in the area of Mordovia. Perhaps there were others. It is impossible to say with any certainty where and how long Bishop Nicholas was imprisoned in each of these camps. He was transferred around thirty times in the next eight years.

The concentration camps were often separated by thousands of miles. To get from camp to camp, it was often necessary to travel for weeks at a time, and to be crowded into enclosed freight cars formerly used to transport cattle, to freeze in winter and bake in the summer, to endure cruel treatment from the criminal element among the prisoners, and inhumane treatment from camp guards. When the train station at which the prisoners arrived was distant from the gulag, the journey had to be completed by foot. The transfers themselves caused extraordinary suffering.

Bishop Charnetsky was imprisoned first in the Mariinsk laager (about 4,000 miles east of Moscow). Towards the end of 1947 he was transferred to Vorkuta. Vorkuta is the final station on the Pechora railway line, and lies within the Arctic Circle, with temperatures that drop to fifty degrees Celsius below zero. There the winter is ten months long, with no evidence of the sun. Below one and a half meters the earth is always frozen. The short summer cannot defrost it. The Vorkuta region is a rich coal-mining area. The weather conditions were so harsh that no one was ever willing to go and work there. Now the prisoners offered a new labor force. Bishop Charnetsky was also in the camps in Mordovia. Often he was transferred together with Metropolitan Slipyj to these various camps.

The conditions in a laager were very difficult. It was a highly secured compound, surrounded by barbed wire, watchtowers, floodlights, guards with automatic weapons. The food was minimal, between four hundred fifty to six hundred grams of bread a day and some warm broth, literally bread and water. There was a strict regimen of daily order: rising, quick breakfast, assembly, work, midday meal break of an hour, work, supper, and bed. In the morning when the guard-escort would appear at the assembly, the prisoners leave in brigades, hands linked, strictly in groups of five. Accompanied by these armed escorts and their dogs, the brigades go down in the middle of the muddy road, in groups of five, to their place of work in the bush, in the mines. Every day, in the morning and evening, the camp is inspected. Those who remained in the camp worked at various jobs. Invalids also are put to work. Only the seriously ill, who are certified by a doctor as free for that day, are free from work. Amid abusive language, and even physical abuse, work goes on, both inside and outside the camp zone.

The laagers have as their objective two purposes: (1) to remove, and even destroy morally, those whom the bolshevik authorities consider their enemies by reason of religious convictions or political views and (2) to avail themselves of cheap slave labor. In order that the prisoners fulfill these objectives: (1) the prisoners must perform hard labor; (2) the prisoners are deprived of adequate food; and (3) prisoners live under constant terror. There is not only an entire army of police surveillance to contend with; there is also the realization that some prisoners are secret informers. For every infraction of the regimen, the prisoner meets with punishment: incarceration with solitary confinement and a more severe food restriction.

Dr. Anthony Kniazhynsky who was in the laager-camps gives us the above details. He also relates in detail one of his experiences in the concentration camp when he encountered Bishop Charnetsky. It was in the Mariinsk laager. One day, new arrivals came to the camp, among them were Metropolitan Josyf Slipyj, Bishop Nicholas Charnetsky, and Father Peter Verhun. Because of their physical conditions, Bishop Nicholas and Father Peter were categorized as "invalids," while Metropolitan Josyf got light labor.

The three church dignitaries mentioned had recently undergone arrest and interrogation, and sentencing. Whereas I was already recovering from the suffering of the interrogation prison and was beginning to manage to survive, the three of them were still experiencing the mental depression that is inevitable in the bolshevik prison-camp situation. The Metropolitan, for the most part was silent, sought to be alone, and prayed. Bishop Charnetsky openly consoled himself and others around him by repeating that Divine assistance was soon to come because Satan had already reached the peak of his malice. Father Verhun saw everywhere automatic weapons aimed at his head....I, together with other Ukrainians, were quick to come with moral assistance to these distinguished "novices"; this was the greatest role that could be played by concerned fellow-prisoners for these newcomers, who lay trampled and bruised by the boot of the bolshevik oppressor.

There was, at the time, starvation in the Mariinsk camp, so we who had been there longer, secretly organized a plan of supplementing their nourishment from our meager funds, buying "on the sly" anything that was available from provisions brought to the camp. Thus it was that they survived, those who were in danger of death from exhaustion....

Having rested and recuperated a little, Bishop Charnetsky did not sit around idly in the barracks. He wandered about the camp zone in search of the most abandoned. Every day he would come up to me, look in my face, and find some words of comfort for me, as well as he could. Sometimes he would sit beside me, ask me how my health was, how I was feeling, and other things which were most important to us, and often he would say "It will get better: for sure it will get better. God will not put up with this. We must believe, because faith can work wonders!" Here he would, with deep conviction, cite words from Holy Scripture, and assure everyone that "so it must be"....

The people from Volyn who were in the camp would flock to him. They knew his best, from better times. "Have you seen our Father today?" they would ask me, when on any given day they had not been able to see him; "Do you think he might be ill?"…He was such a precious human being, without whom it would have been difficult to survive. He knew everyone by name, and everyone was precious to him. This was his greatest charism, a gift from God. It was no wonder that Bishop Charnetsky was forever surrounded by these unfortunate people, because only from him would they receive word of comfort and consolation….

I and many others, among them these mentioned hierarchs, were eventually transferred to another laager-camp….And here Bishop Charnetsky found more unfortunates who needed his good word. Here I saw him more often among people, and now he no longer was empty-handed. Someone from our own country sent him, from time to time, small parcels, which he distributed among the unfortunate. Sometimes he would come to me, too, and slip into my hands at least a couple of pieces of sugar, or a head of garlic, murmuring, "Whatever the house is rich in…."

Soon there came a renewed assault on the Catholic clergy. All the Catholic priests were rounded up in a staging area and processed for transfer. In order, however, for the occasion to "provide profit," all those who might possess something worthwhile were detained in a criminals' barracks where, during the night, they were robbed. We prisoners thought that Bishop Nicholas Charnetsky would not survive much longer, but he would yet have to drink deep, to the very bottom, of the martyr's chalice.

Another fellow-prisoner, Father Pietro Leoni, S.J., met Bishop Charnetsky and Metropolitan Slipyj in the transit prison at Kirov. He describes his stay there.

This was the filthiest prison that I had the occasion to see. Bedbugs, roaches, had multiplied by the millions, and at night it was impossible to defend oneself against them because the room was in total darkness. Only when they portioned out supper did they bring a miserable oil lamp, which they immediately took away, leaving us at the mercy of the parasites which, in the darkness become insatiable and more aggressive. The three nights that I spent in that prison were a veritable martyrdom.

The next day they left by train. Along the way in Pechora, the bishops were told to get out.

Dr. Franz Grobauer was another fellow-prisoner who also met Bishop Charnetsky and Metropolitan Slipyj in a transport in the Komi Autonomous Soviet Socialist Republic in the fall of 1947. They were on their way to Inta, Komi, to the coal mines. He writes:

The bishop was gracious to everyone, and always reminded me of the Saint Nicholas of my childhood. Charnetsky was, alas, too trusting, so that certain unscrupulous individuals often took advantage of him in the most brutal fashion. In the aforementioned transport there were, besides the so-called "political" prisoners, also criminal prisoners; these would rob every fellow-prisoner, even if he possessed the smallest trifle. The bishop carried with him a large sack, on which he used to sit. One time, several young criminals pushed him off the sack, onto the floor, and the last possessions of this prince of the Church were gone. Unforgettable was the reaction of the bishop: "The Lord gives; the Lord takes away."

During the months of the long journey, I lay near the bishop on the cold floor of the freight car. We had enough free time to converse about everything. Unfortunately, the conversation was not easy for me, because Bishop Charnetsky was hard of hearing in one ear and, because of the numerous spies that were planted among the prisoners in every one of the freight cars, I did not care to speak too loudly. Finally, we ended up talking to each other in Latin.

Dr. Grobauer describes their arrival in Inta on December 5, 1947, on a stormy and bitterly cold day. They had to walk through deep snow and in their physical state it would have been easy to just disappear in this snow. With much effort they arrived at the laager. In the laager, since all three (Metropolitan Josyf, Bishop Nicholas, and Dr. Grobauer) were sick, they were sent to the barracks' hospital. There for months they shared the same bed. In a letter Dr. Grobauer describes Bishop Nicholas in this way:

In contrast to Slipyj who was, on the surface, rather reserved, Charnetsky always strove to keep contact with his fellow-prisoners, among whom there were many from Western Ukraine, and these regarded Charnetsky very highly. They secretly went for confession to him, and also he frequently blessed the rosaries that they made from string.

Charnetsky more frequently received parcels from Lviv, gifts of love, which consisted of dried fruit, tobacco, biscuits, and raisins (dried grapes). The latter had a special purpose: soaked in a cup of water, they provided wine for the Divine Liturgy....

The bishop [Charnetsky] was, one night, forcibly relieved of his precious ecclesiastical memento (his panagia, or bishop's medal)....Charnetsky was forever reminding me that, in the event that somehow I gained my freedom,

I must reveal all the sufferings which the representatives of the Catholic Church had to endure—and continue to endure—in the Soviet prisons and concentration camps.

Soon their paths parted and they were sent to various camps. Dr. Grobauer also mentioned in his letter that some criticized the behavior of Bishop Charnetsky because he was approachable to everybody and sought contact with his fellow-prisoners. True, some criminal types exploited this and even robbed him; however, this attitude toward everyone in the camp called forth in those who were suffering misfortune a great deal of trust and confidence. Many even came to him secretly for confession. For those imprisoned in the bolshevik camps, where the entire environment was full of suffering and pain, and evoked in the prisoners only hopelessness, a priest—or a bishop—by his accessibility and his goodness, and by his spirit of joy, was a healing balsam, as it were, for the wounded hearts of the imprisoned. Just such a healing balsam for the pain-filled hearts of the prisoners in the bolshevik laager-camps was Bishop Charnetsky.

While in the camps in Mordovia, Bishop Charnetsky encountered numerous priests. Among them was Father Vasyl Kurylas. He describes how he and other priests would celebrate the Divine Liturgy.

I celebrated the Divine Liturgy every day, before wake-up call, at my plank bed. The prosphora (liturgical bread) was sent to us from home, and the wine we made from raisins, also sent to us from home. One priest helped another. For a long time, maybe a year, in one of the camps in Mordovia, I brought Holy Communion (under one Species) every day to Father Charnetsky, the Redemptorist bishop, until he finally ventured to celebrate the Divine Liturgy himself.

The Divine Liturgy was a source of great strength. It was difficult though not impossible to celebrate it in the camp. One had to think out the possibilities and plan ahead for the actualization of celebrating the Divine Liturgy. Dr. Kniazhynsky described how Bishop Charnetsky celebrated the Divine Liturgy in the camp where he, the doctor, was incarcerated. In this camp there were bunk beds, made of planks, on which the prisoners slept. Dr. Kniazhynsky had a bed in the vicinity of Kyr Nicholas. Very early, before the bell—or rather, the rail iron—sounded to awaken the prisoners, the bishop would secretly celebrate the Divine Liturgy at his own bedside, while Dr. Kniazhynsky, from his bed, would keep watch to see if any of the supervisors were coming. In the medical barracks it might be possible, if the supervisors were trustworthy, to celebrate the Divine Liturgy very easily early in the morning. The Divine Liturgy and prayer were the invincible sources of strength that maintained our suffering servant in his heroic bravery and peace of soul, full of profound trust in Divine Providence.

Spoon on which Bishop Nicholas celebrated the Divine Liturgy in prison.

The spoon upon which the bishop celebrated the Divine Liturgy was given to a Redemptorist from Canada during his visit to Ukraine in 1967. This very precious relic brings many thoughts to mind. It was on this broken spoon that Bishop Charnetsky offered, in the Service of God, the bloodless sacrifice of Jesus Christ—the same sacrifice that Christ offered in a bloody manner on Golgotha. Golgotha and the bolshevik laager! What a similarity! From this spoon one can read about Bishop Charnetsky's entire life of suffering, about his way of the cross in the bolshevik prisons and camps. This broken spoon was, for everyone imprisoned, both altar and church. But that Church cannot be broken by any earthly power, because within it lives Christ: Christ lives in his saints, in those who profess Him—Christ the Redeeming Conqueror, who continues to call out: "Be not afraid! I have conquered the world!" (John 16:23).

The bishop was transferred many times. Scattered reports are given by eyewitnesses that they saw him in this camp or in that camp and at various times. In the end, his last imprisonment was in Mordovia. The bolshevik authorities brought him to Mordovia when the bishop began to fail markedly in health. Here conditions were somewhat better, and they brought some change to a person whose health was already so ruined. The bishop, however, was already hopelessly sick: three times he had had jaundice, in addition to dropsy and other illnesses. They had given up hope for his recovery and had already prepared the prison burial clothes for him. However, the Communist authorities sent him off to Lviv in 1956: they did not want him to die in a concentration camp, because his death would create certain unpleasantness for the bolshevik government. Kyr Nicholas was so sick that it was hard for him to walk, so they did not send him alone, but with him they released a priest and another prisoner to accompany him.

His Last Years

After his release, immediately after his arrival in Lviv, Bishop Charnetsky had to spend time in the hospital on Piotr Skarga Avenue. Thanks to the attentive care of the Sisters of St. Vincent who served this hospital, the bishop recovered almost miraculously, and went to live, together with one confrere, in the Kulparkiv section of Lviv. The living quarters of Kyr Nicholas were small, consisting of one room and a kitchen.

The bolshevik authorities, even now, did not allow him

Inside Bishop Charnetsky's residence after his release from prison.

any priestly function. Early every morning, however, the bishop celebrated the Divine Liturgy in a corner of his room, on an ordinary table, behind a curtain, secretly, so as not to attract the attention of the police who kept an eye on him. The Redemptorist brother who lived with him assisted at the liturgy, and he then went to work in a factory, so that with his pay he could support himself and the bishop.

Bishop Nicholas, in his solitude and holiness of life, was a support to his confreres. After all the illnesses and the imprisonments that he had endured, the bishop was able, during these final years, secretly to ordain thirteen priests, and in this way to contribute to the preservation of the Ukrainian Catholic Church. Many of those he ordained themselves were soon imprisoned by the Soviets and had to endure prisons and laager-camps. The Ukrainian Catholic Church was declared an illegal entity by the Soviet Union. Through a pseudo-synod in March 1946, the Ukrainian Catholic Church was liquidated and "joined" to the Russian Orthodox State Church.

Bishop Nicholas shortly before his death.

When the companion who lived with the bishop died, Kyr Nicholas was left alone in his solitary room. He read, he prayed, and his only diversion was that old friends visited him: except for that he spent his time in prayer, both day and night. He endured his pains bravely, completely submissive to God, seeing in everything Divine Providence. Those who visited the bishop tell that they saw him in the state of ecstasy.

His health, however, was no longer there: the long years of

bolshevik enslavement in various prisons and camps, the cruel treatment he had had to endure, had completely sapped the strength of the bishop's powerful physique. The bishop became like a living skeleton—his mouth twisted, his beard completely white, dark eyes shining in depths of his sunken sockets: his entire appearance giving evidence of his great suffering. Still, he forever maintained a serenity of spirit, characterized by peace.

In January 1959, Bishop Charnetsky became ill and was taken to the hospital on Piotr Skarga Avenue. He underwent an operation for cancer of the intestine. The operation was successful, but soon after there was a relapse. On April 2, 1959, at 9:00 P.M., Bishop Nicholas peacefully fell asleep in the Lord. The last words of the deceased bishop were sighs to the Mother of Perpetual Help: Kyr Nicholas had a deep devotion to the Most Holy Mother of God and a heart full of love for her.

A Redemptorist from Lviv described these events.

That same night, his body was transferred to his dwelling at #7 Vechirnia Avenue, where he had lived. The Ukrainian Catholic community, his family by blood and spirit, busied themselves with preparations for the funeral.

On Friday, April 3, I went to pay my respects to the deceased and to pray. Kyr Mykolay (Nicholas) lay on a simple catafalque, dressed in a monastic robe, purple cloak, embroidered stole, omofor, and mitre. In his powerful hands he had a small cross and chotky-beads. The catafalque was surrounded with live flowers in vases. Many people came to pray, to take their leave of the deceased, to kiss the feet or the vestment of the deceased bishop. Everyone cried.

The funeral took place on Saturday, April 4. It began at 3:30 and ended at 6:30. The entire funeral service in the Byzantine rite was sung in the room where the deceased had lived; after that, Father Karl Jastrzembski, a Latin priest from the cathedral, came to preside and conclude the funeral. The coffin was carried in turn by priests and brother-monks dressed in civilian clothes, along the muddy road, about two kilometers, to the Kul'parkivsky cemetery. Along the way they sang Sviaty Bozhe (Holy God), *and the people recited prayers along the entire way, interspersed with sobbing and weeping of the people. At the cemetery the coffin was opened for the "final greeting," and the prescribed prayer-stanzas were sung, and then the panachyda. The Latin priest intoned* Salve Regina (Hail, Queen), *and we sang* Vichnaia pamiat' (Eternal Memory). *The coffin was black. A large box was put inside the grave, and the coffin placed inside the box. The deceased bishop was buried in the Kul'parkivsky cemetery by the field road, a little beyond the graves of the deceased from the hospital for the mentally ill. There was no obstructions whatsoever to the funeral; everything took place normally, with a great concourse of people. People cried, because everyone loved him, and they grieved greatly for the deceased bishop.*

The body of Bishop Charnetsky did not rest very long in the Kul'parkivsky cemetery. The city of Lviv began to expand in the direction of the cemetery, so this cemetery was expropriated; anyone who so desired was allowed to transfer his deceased to the cemetery at Lychakiv. In November 1969, the bishop's body was transferred to the Lychakivsky cemetery. Daily since that time people have been coming to his grave asking the holy bishop for favors. Many signs and wonders have already occurred at his grave side or through his intercession.

CHRONOLOGY OF
BISHOP NICHOLAS CHARNETSKY, C.SS.R.

December 14, 1884: Nicholas Charnetsky is born in the village of Semakivci, district of Horodenka in Halychyna, Western Ukraine. Nicholas is the first of nine children.

1890: Nicholas begins school in Tovmach.

1896–1904: Nicholas attends the *gymnasia* (high school) in Stanyslaviv. He lives in a residence for students attached to the cathedral church.

1904: Nicholas begins Theological Studies at *De Propaganda Fide* University.

October 2, 1909: Nicholas is ordained to the priesthood by Bishop Gregory Khomyshyn in Stanyslaviv. He returns to Rome to obtain a doctorate in theology.

Fall 1910: Father Nicholas becomes professor of philosophy and dogmatic theology in the seminary in Stanyslaviv. He is also the spiritual director.

1918: Two Redemptorists visit the seminary in Stanyslaviv. Encouraged through the spiritual direction of Father Nicholas, several students joined the Congregation.

August 1919: Father Charnetsky begins his novitiate with the Redemptorists in Zboisk.

October 16, 1920: Father Nicholas makes his first profession of vows as a Redemptorist.

1920–1922: Father Nicholas is assigned to the new Redemptorist monastery in Stanyslaviv.

1922–1926: He teaches at the Redemptorist Minor Seminary in Zboisk. He also becomes the Assistant Novice Master in Holosko.

April 3, 1926: Father Charnetsky goes to Volyn to work among the Orthodox and bring them into re-union with the Catholic Church.

Fall 1926: Father Nicholas founds the first Redemptorist house in Kostopil, Volyn. Later, in 1927, they are forced to abandon this home.

September 11, 1927: Father Charnetsky founds a new home in Kovel, Volyn.

January 16, 1931: Father Nicholas is named titular bishop of Lebedos, appointed as Apostolic Visitator of the Ukrainian Catholics in Volyn.

February 8, 1931: He is consecrated bishop in the Redemptorist Church of St. Alphonsus in Rome by Bishop Gregory Khomyshyn of Stanyslaviv.

September 8, 1931: The monastery in Kovel was canonically erected as a Redemptorist monastery and becomes the bishop's residence.

Fall 1931: Bishop Nicholas reactivates the seminary in Dubno.

1931–1939: Bishop Nicholas does pastoral work for the people of Volyn, Polisia, Pidliasia, and Belorussia. He ordains Redemptorist seminarians and others. He participates in Church Unity Conferences almost every year.

September 1939: With the beginning of the Second World War, Bishop Nicholas is unable to return to Volyn and is confined to Lviv.

December 22, 1939: Together with Metropolitan Sheptytsky and Bishop Nicetas Budka, he secretly co-consecrates Josyf Slypyj as bishop with the right of succession to the Metropolitan See.

1939–1941: During the Soviet occupation of Halychyna, Bishop Nicholas engages in apostolic work in Lviv, especially in the confessional and in serving in the church that was attached to the monastery.

June 1941: The Germans occupy Halychyna. Again Bishop Charnetsky is not allowed into Volyn.

July 1944: Halychyna again goes under Soviet occupation. Oppression and persecution of the Ukrainian Catholic Church begins.

April 11, 1945: Bishop Nicholas Charnetsky is arrested by Soviet security forces while at the monastery on Zyblikevych Avenue.

1945–1946: He is imprisoned in Kiev. At first he is sentenced to five years of hard labor for being an "agent of the Vatican." He is sent to Mariinsk, about 4,000 miles east of Moscow.

1947–1956: Bishop Nicholas is sent to Vorkuta and is frequently transferred from camp to camp: Kirov, Inta, Pechora, and Mordovia.

1956: He is released from prison and confined to Lviv.

1959: In January he again becomes gravely ill and is hospitalized.

April 2, 1959: Bishop Nicholas Charnetsky falls asleep in the Lord. He is first buried in Kul'parkivsky Cemetery. In 1969 his remains are moved to Lychakivsky Cemetery.

Chapter 2

*V*ASYL (BASIL) VSEVOLOD VELYCHKOVSKY, C.Ss.R.

1903–1973

B lessed Basil's life spanned the early years of this century, the turmoil of the two World Wars, the Soviet occupation of Ukraine, imprisonment in slave-labor camps, and, finally, a visit to Canada at the invitation of Metropolitan Maksym Hermaniuk, during which he died on June 30, 1973.

Father John Sianchuk, C.Ss.R., recalls meeting Bishop Basil during the bishop's final trip to Canada:

> *I was entering my second year of theology when I met Blessed Basil Velychovsky in our monastery in Yorkton, Saskatchewan, in July of 1972. I saw a quite large built man with a white beard and peaceful eyes. He was a soft-spoken man. My confreres whispered to me that he was a dynamic preacher, but that Soviet prisons had broken him. As we seminarians sang for him, he began to cry. Later, at our evening gathering, he said little but again easily succumbed to tears. Only now do I understand, in part, the reason for the tears.*

He had only recently been released from the Soviet prisons. He was exiled from his native country Ukraine. Here he was in the "free world" where the Ukrainian Catholic Church was not outlawed. He had left others—bishops and priests in his place before his last arrest by the KGB, but the persecution in his native land was still in full force. We, who were with him that evening, had no sense of the tremendous contrast between these two worlds. We thought he would rejoice to be "free," but instead his heart was heavily wounded having seen the great destruction the church was undergoing in Ukraine. Blessed Basil cried with the tears of Jesus looking upon Jerusalem and seeing the blindness of his own people to the truth, for he looked upon us and saw that we do not understand the price of the Cross.

He lived in Canada for less than a year from that time. Overcome from the tortures he had endured over the past years, and suffering from a slow-working drug with which he was induced before he left prison, he fell asleep in the Lord on June 30, 1973.

HIS FAMILY

Basil Vsevolod Velychkovsky was born on June 1, 1903, in Stanyslaviv (now Ivano-Frankivsk) in Western Ukraine. He was the eldest of three children, having two sisters, Vera and Barbara. His father, Volodymyr, was a priest serving as an assistant at the cathedral when Basil was born. Basil came from a long line of priests, including his grandfather, Father Julian, who was among the first to preach in Ukrainian.

Basil's father was orphaned at a young age. He enrolled in law school, and, as he needed money, he took a job tutoring the children of a priest's family, Father Nicholas Teodorovych. This Father Nicholas was a zealous priest, and in his home reigned a spirit of devotion. All the Teodorovych children had religious vocations. Two sons entered the Basilian Order, and two became diocesan priests. Daughter Irene became superior for the Basilian Sisters. Maria, married at first to a diocesan priest, Anna (Basil's mother), and Father Nicholas's wife all joined the Basilian Sisters after the deaths of their husbands. Through the influence of this family, the young law student Volodymyr eventually entered the seminary.

Since Basil was raised in a priestly family, from his early life he lived in an atmosphere of prayer. Describing his early life Bishop Basil says this:

> *My father was a zealous and holy priest, and my mother was a devout and exemplary mother and wife, a shining example for the home and parish. I remember Father, from morning on, always praying, meditating, confessing, celebrating Divine Liturgy. He never missed praying his breviary and rosary. Before nightfall he went to church with the entire family to visit the Most Holy Eucharist. Every day Mother assisted at the Divine Liturgy and received Holy Communion with us children and the household. Mother had a good heart. She took in the abandoned and the orphaned and raised them, assisting them in setting up their own families or entering a monastery. I remember how once she took in a poor blind girl and cared for her until her death.*

It was in such an atmosphere that the first seeds of a vocation to religious life were born in the young Basil.

His Early Years

Basil was baptized in the cathedral of Stanyslaviv where his father served. Soon after his father was transferred to the parish in Shuparets, in the district of Borschiv, Western Ukraine. There Basil grew up and received First Holy Communion. His education was sporadic. At first he was taught at home. At age eight he

Interior of parish church in Shuparets where Blessed Basil was raised, received his first holy Communion, and where he celebrated his first Divine Liturgy.

attended primary school for a few years in his grandfather's town of Probizhnia. In May 1911, Basil attended a retreat with his mother. At his mother's request, the preacher dedicated Basil to the Mother of God. Basil placed great importance on this event in his life. He experienced the protection and intercession of Mary on several occasions. She led him to join the Redemptorists who honor her as the Mother of Perpetual Help. She also became his great strength during his imprisonment.

After finishing primary school in 1913–1914, he went to the Institute of St. Josaphat's, a secondary school in Buchach under the care of the Basilians. Then World War I broke out. The military front line was at the Dniester River just a few miles away. Formal schooling was impossible, so Basil returned home and was again taught there, this time by theology students. Once the front had moved further east, Basil was sent to school in

Altar of the Mother of God in Probizhnia where young Basil was dedicated to her at the age of seven.

Horodenka on the Austrian side of the Dniester River for one year.

In 1918, an internal war was brewing between the Poles and Ukrainians. Basil left school and joined the *Striltsi*, "the Riflemen," fighting to keep Western Ukraine independent. Eastern Ukraine had fallen to the Russians after the Revolution. While with the *Striltsi*, Basil was assigned office work, so he never went to the front. Thus, though often amid great danger, he remained unhurt.

Upon the defeat of the *Striltsi* in November 1919, Basil was arrested by the Polish army. He was condemned to be shot and forced to dig his own grave. But before the grave was dug, another officer commuted the punishment, sentencing him to hard labor in a laager-camp in Zolochiv, Ukraine. Basil received monetary help from home and soon escaped. He went to a Basilian monastery where his aunt, Sister Mary-Monica (Maria), was superior. He was a "wanted man" and was hidden in a Studite monastery in Univ. But his situation was very dangerous, so he headed for the Czech border to escape. At the border he was arrested again. However, the guards were unaware that he had escaped from prison camp, so they sent him for questioning to his home district in Borshchiv. Because of the good relations between his father and the authorities of the town, Basil was released. Finally, in 1920–1921, Basil completed his studies in Stanyslaviv.

HIS RELIGIOUS LIFE

In the fall of 1921, Basil was accepted into the major seminary in Lviv and was enrolled in the first year of Theological Institute. He should have entered the seminary in Stanyslaviv because he belonged to that eparchy, but this diocese had compulsory celibacy, and he did not wish to follow that course. However, in Lviv, married clergy were acceptable.

In the seminary, he was able to live the same deeper spiritual life as he had before the war—regular Confession, Holy Communion, meditation, visits to the chapel, and so on. At the seminary, many men were in attendance there because it was the only place to obtain a higher education. The influence of these students was not always positive. Sometimes Basil followed their bad influence, sneaking into the city, smoking heavily, and even taking an occasional drink. However, he never fell into serious sin. He says of himself in his *Autobiography*:

Ukrainian Catholic Major Seminary in Lviv where Blessed Basil took his theology.

In spite of my light-heartedness and inclination toward
evil, Divine Grace, without any merit of mine, saved me
from dangerous proximate occasions, and sometimes when
such occasions occurred, saved me from big bad falls.

He entered the major seminary in Lviv with the intention of being a married priest like his father. However, during a retreat in his third year, he made a decision to accept the celibate state. Basil wrote: "This decision was not the result of some unexpected shock, some inconsiderate, insensitive strength, but the fruit of the imperceptible, sweet, powerful, indomitable influence of divine grace, God's love."

Basil approached Metropolitan Andrew Sheptytsky the next week to request ordination to the diaconate. The Metropolitan asked him to reconsider, but Basil was ordained a deacon and committed his life to celibacy.

In the summer of 1924 while visiting his aunt Sister Mary-Monica, they traveled to the Redemptorist monastery in Zboisk.

Basil's aunt said she had a spiritual matter to discuss with the rector, Father Joseph Schrijvers, C.Ss.R. Basil waited outside smoking a cigarette and was then called in. Meeting Father Schrijvers for the first time, he was greeted very paternally and warmly with these words:

Good, good. I accept you into our monastery. Go home, for a little while, for vacation, and on August 1 come to Holosko for novitiate. You may smoke in your room, but one less cigarette every day, because we do not smoke.

Basil was surprised at being admitted into the monastery *without ever even requesting it,* but he did not question this turn of events and took it as Divine Providence. Soon the Metropolitan released him from the seminary and Basil began his novitiate. Upon entering novitiate Basil freely gave up smoking once and for all.

Novitiate was a time of intense prayer and physical activity. The new monastery needed much work, especially the grounds. For Basil, the year passed quickly. With great joy he professed his vows in the Redemptorist Congregation on August 29, 1925.

Since he was already a deacon, he was assigned to teach in the minor seminary in Zboisk. On the staff also was Father Nicholas Charnetsky.

Deacon Basil completed his theology and on October 9, 1925, in the monastery Church of Zboisk he received the great Mystery of the Priesthood at the hands of Bishop Joseph Bocian, Bishop of Lutsk. Father Basil was filled with joy on October 14, the feast of the Protection of the Mother of God, as he celebrated the Divine Liturgy with his family in his hometown of Shuparets.

In speaking about his vocation Father Basil says this:

I told myself then that, if there were not among us the missionary Congregation of the Most Holy Redeemer, I would have entered the monastery of the Studite Order. I have many links with the Order of St. Basil the Great. It is dear and close; seven of my closest family members are there; I, too, was for a short time, because of the War, in the St. Josaphat gymnasia at Buchach. But to enter the monastic life of that Basilian Order was never the inclination of my heart—why, I do not know myself.

But I am a priest of the Congregation of the Most Holy Redeemer because such is the will of God, such is the calling of our Savior for me: here is my place, where I must accomplish the mission given to me by God, and here I must, with Jesus, be the sacrifice for our Church and our People.

BASIL'S APOSTOLIC WORK

Father Basil taught at the minor seminary from 1925 to 1927. Although he taught many subjects, his heart was in the preaching apostolate. He prepared mission sermons and took every opportunity to preach the Word of God. He had a gift for preaching. Soon he began visiting villages and towns in Halychyna, giving missions and various spiritual exercises. In order to devote himself more to the missions, he was assigned to the monastery in Stanyslaviv.

This Redemptorist house was a true missionary center. Many from the town as well as neighboring villagers came to the monastery chapel. In addition, the monastery was the center of the Confraternity of the Mother of Perpetual Help.

In 1926, a new field of apostolic work opened for the Redemptorists in Volyn, where many Ukrainian Catholics had settled after World War I. Also, many Orthodox desired to return to Church Union, which the government of Moscow had repressed there in the nineteenth century. This new apostolate was initiated by Fathers Nicholas Charnetsky and Gregory Shyshkovych at the invitation of the local Latin-Rite Ordinary, Bishop Adolph Szelazek.

In 1928, Father Shyshkovych left for Canada and Father Basil arrived at the Redemptorist monastery in Kovel on November 16 to replace him. Father Basil immediately began visiting the settlers from Halychyna scattered throughout Volyn and serving the Orthodox newly reunited with the Catholic Church. Much work was needed among the settlers. Often they had not seen a priest for a long time. During his visits, he would celebrate Divine Liturgies, preach, hear confessions, teach, baptize the children, marry adults, visit the sick, establish cemeteries, build chapels, and so on. Through his inspiring preaching, Father Basil saw many Orthodox parishes become reunited with the Catholic Church. He established the Confraternity of the Mother of Perpetual Help in these parishes as well.

He was close to the people sharing with them the poor conditions. Often it was necessary to stay and celebrate the Divine Services in poor village huts. Father Basil gladly embraced these difficulties. People took him to heart, recognizing his generous love, affability, humility, and genuine devotion.

Like other priests in his family, Father Basil preached in Ukrainian rather than Polish. This endeared him to the people from Halychyna and to the Orthodox. But the Polish government accused him of being a political agitator, alleging that his missionary work had Ukrainian nationalist motivation. The underhanded struggle against his work in Volyn, including protests to the Apostolic See, were so powerful that it seemed prudent to recall Father Basil from Volyn in 1935.

Father Basil was transferred back to Stanyslaviv, where he was able to preach missions. The missions were ordinarily ten days in length and were great religious renewals. Thousands partook in the solemn procession through the villages, carrying large mission crosses. Metropolitan Andrew Sheptytsky invited Father Basil to give missions in the main churches in the city of Lviv.

In 1938, Father Basil was named superior of the monastery in Stanyslaviv. The Fathers there had been collecting funds for a new church in honor of Our Mother of Perpetual Help. But the commencement of World War II and the Soviet occupation of Halychyna in 1939 prevented the church from being built. The small Redemptorist chapel served as a hub of religious activity.

From this plot of land where Our Mother of Perpetual Help monastery formerly stood, Blessed Basil led a missionary life from 1935 to 1941, much of it with Blessed Zenon Kovalyk. They preached ten-day missions throughout the region.

DURING THE SECOND WORLD WAR

In early 1940, the Soviets wanted to force the Redemptorists out of the monastery. When the people found this out they protested en masse to the authorities. When the Soviets saw so many ready to shed their blood to prevent them from occupying the monastery they dropped their plans.

On the Feast of Our Mother of Perpetual Help that year, Father Basil planned the usual procession through the streets with the icon. Since the city was occupied by the Soviets, this procession would be deemed illegal. But, when Father Basil saw the crowd on Our Lady's feast day—over 20,000—he decided to go ahead with the celebration. The procession was itself a sermon on the power of the eucharistic Jesus and the blessing of Our Mother of Perpetual Help as they paraded through the streets in full sight of the Communists. Some tried to disrupt the proces-

Father Basil in 1929.

sion, but all attempts failed. Father Basil preached a solemn sermon on the triumphant power of Jesus and Mary. The people lingered long afterward, as if caught up in prayerful exaltation.

Days later Father Basil was interrogated by the NKVD, the Soviet's internal security police force. When asked why he organized this religious procession, he tells about his answer in his *Autobiography:*

*Beyond the borders, they are writing that you are perse-
cuting us. If I had not organized the procession it would
have been taken as proof of such persecution. I knew that
you would not give permission; however, in order that those
beyond the borders would not have an excuse to speak about
persecution, I organized the procession without permission—I did it for the sake of your prestige and reputation.*

This cunning answer caught the interrogator by surprise and
he had to agree with the priest.

Suddenly another NKVD officer entered and began to abuse
Father Basil. He threw himself at the priest, fists flailing at his
head. Father Basil was taken aback by the wild and rabid attack.
The officers screamed: "Confess, admit it, or you go immediately against the wall like a mongrel dog! Admit it, scoundrel!"

Father Basil looked at his attacker and said firmly yet calmly:
"To this uncultured man I will answer not a single word!"

In his *Autobiography*, Father Basil describes what happens
next:

*I turned away from him, sat with my hands on the back of
the chair, and began to say the rosary, holding it high in
my hands. He continued to shout. My head rang. I was
almost unconscious. I just kept praying "Hail Mary." Of
that prayer I am aware, nothing else.*

A different interrogator took over, this one more a gentle-
man. Father Basil spoke with him, signed some papers, and was
released.

Because Father Basil was well-known and popular in Stanyslaviv, the NKVD were afraid to arrest him. Yet he was warned
by an NKVD officer that he would not be arrested because of
the support of the people, but that once he sets foot out of
Stanyslaviv he would be swiftly arrested. So Father Basil continued his apostolic work there in the city.

Ancient church of St. Nicholas in Kamianets-Podilsk where Blessed Basil preached and celebrated the Divine Services.

In June 1941, the Soviets retreated as the Germans entered and occupied Halychyna. At first, the Germans were seen as liberators by the Ukrainians, but soon that perception changed. During the German occupation there was, however, greater freedom for the church. Metropolitan Andrew Sheptytsky asked Father Basil to go to Greater Ukraine where people were asking for a Catholic priest. So, in September 1941, Father Basil set out for Kamianets Podilsk, fifteen miles or so east of Halychyna.

In the first town on his journey, Kudrynets, just across the river, he consecrated a newly built church, confessed all who requested, baptized hundreds of children, and celebrated the Divine Services. When the neighboring village heard there was a priest nearby, they brought him to their village where he encountered a similar scene.

He went to the next village doing the same, and so on, until he reached Kamianets where he was greeted by folks who had long awaited a priest. The Ukrainian Catholic Church was abol-

Inside of the church of St. Nicholas in Kamianets-Podilsk.

ished there in 1795 and Russian Orthodoxy introduced. His experience in Volyn had prepared him for this work, developing in him a great sensitivity to the Orthodox mentality. The people warmly and enthusiastically welcomed him. He chose to work in the small unoccupied ancient stone Church of St. Nicholas, and people flocked to the place.

The first evening at the Vesper Vigil Service for the Feast of the Exaltation of the Holy Cross, Father Basil preached about the opening of the Greek-Catholic-Orthodox parish: "…a parish as in the days of your grandparents and great-grandparents.

Those who wish to become parishioners, may do so through Confession and Holy Communion. I will immediately begin hearing confessions. If anything is unclear, then tomorrow come to the residence for further explanation. And now you may all go home."

He then gave a summary of the next day's schedule; however, no one left. When he asked if anyone wanted to go to confession, everyone responded. He confessed for hours, well into the night, and began again at dawn. After experiencing the Divine Liturgy with these people, Father Basil was convinced of the power of God's grace that had caused such a great devotion among these people.

Unfortunately, this mission was short lived. Soon the German authorities heard of this work and gave Father Basil twenty-four hours to leave or face a firing squad. Fortunately, he left unnoticed and safely crossed the Zbruch River back to Halychyna. He returned to Lviv.

In 1942, Father Basil became superior of the Redemptorist monastery in Ternopil. He arrived at the end of June and was there until the end of July 1943. During that time, the bolshevik front was far away, so he could go out on missions. Toward the end of the Great Fast in 1943, he organized a men's retreat. At the end of this retreat everyone went to confession and Holy Communion. These participating were the doctors, teachers, lawyers, judges, and civic officials of Ternopil. The event made a great impression on people who saw their leaders renewed in the faith. In the summer of 1943, Father Basil returned to Stanyslaviv and Lviv.

INTO THE JAWS OF DEATH

By fall 1944, the Russians were again approaching Halychyna, pushing the Germans back. Ukrainian Catholics knew that persecutions experienced earlier in the War would intensify. The Redemptorist superior abandoned Ternopil. But the Provincial

Church of the Dormition of the Mother of God in Ternopil where Blessed Basil went in 1944 and stayed until his first arrest on July 26, 1945.

felt concerned about the Soviets finding an empty monastery, so Father Basil volunteered to be present when the Russians arrived. The Provincial reluctantly allowed him to go, realizing that great danger awaited.

Father Basil obtained a ticket from Lviv to Ternopil, but the train only went halfway because of the advancing front. So he hitched a ride in a military car to the outskirts and completed the trip on foot. The shelling of the city had already begun and it was being evacuated. He was allowed to enter only to retrieve documents from the monastery. But, of course, he had no intention of leaving. He made his way to the Redemptorist monastery and found a few confreres there who were happy he had come.

All Redemptorists ignored the evacuation order, and served those who stayed behind. Appointed superior of the monastery again, he began doing limited missionary work in various towns nearby. Meanwhile the NKVD waited for an opportunity to arrest him.

HIS ARREST AND TRAIL

On July 26, 1945, after all the bishops of the Ukrainian Catholic Church were arrested, the NKVD came for Father Basil. He considered escaping, but after praying the Hail Mary, it became clear that the most honorable thing was to place himself into the hands of the Soviets. The head of the NKVD asked how he felt about the unification of the Greek (Ukrainian) Catholic Church with the Russian Orthodox Church. He replied resolutely in the negative. When asked if he would be united with the Russian Orthodox Church, he replied: "No. Never! Under any circumstances."

The officer responded by advising Father Basil to think about his answer carefully since his life was on the line. He threatened Father Basil by saying that he either subscribed to Russian Orthodoxy or else he would not be allowed to leave alive.

Father Basil replied by saying:

Your efforts are of no avail. Your words are useless. You are wasting your time. I have said No once and for all; you can kill me, but you shall get from me no other word.

From the tone of Father Basil's voice, the NKVD interrogator deduced that the priest's words were resolute and irrevocable.

Father Basil spent the next two months in a basement at the KGB headquarters in Chortkiv, an hour from Ternopil. Then he was transferred to Kiev, to the internal prison of the KGB, the Soviet security organization. On route the accompanying officers fell asleep and he had a chance to escape, but he chose not to cause trouble for the guards. In Kiev he was put into a solitary cell little bigger than a locker. Then he was placed into a larger cell containing a bed. The mattress was completely worn so that the straw would sift between the iron rods. He was there for a month then moved to another cell with two others where they slept on the floor.

For nearly two years they interrogated him in order to make

a case against him. The purpose was to force from him a confession of crimes he did not commit. Finally, after scrutinizing all his papers, they found a little pocket calendar printed during the German occupation. It contained an article with intercessory prayers including "save us from the Red band" and "may the Red horde never return to us." Father Basil admitted writing these prayers and was taken to the district court in Kiev where he was found guilty and sentenced to death by a firing squad.

ON DEATH ROW

Father Basil was placed in a cell on death row, the only priest among the inmates. They recognized that he was a priest by his beard and his manner and gave him a place of preference in the cell. The inmates asked him to speak to them since they were all facing death. Father Basil began by teaching them the Our Father and the Hail Mary, which they memorized. Then he taught them about the Holy Mysteries, the sacraments and other subjects. He heard their confessions, celebrated the Divine Liturgy, and they all received Holy Communion. This was repeated as prisoners were taken to their deaths and new ones arrived.

After three months, one night the cell door opened and his name was called. He described this moment in his *Autobiography*:

> I responded with my name, and I heard the reply, "Yes, good. You are to leave, with all your things." I saw an officer and a few guards with automatic weapons.
>
> I rose quickly and began packing. I distributed the produce I had to those who needed it because I knew that I would never return here. I packed the rest of my things, and said a few words of farewell. "Dear brothers, some of you will one day be set free of this prison. I beg you, when you meet anyone from the western districts of Ukraine, tell them—you know my family—that the priest Vely-

chkovsky was shot, killed by a firing squad, for his Catholic Church, for his holy faith. And now, goodbye. May all go well with you..." And I left, looking for the last time upon these good people.

IN THE SOVIET LAAGER-CAMPS

Instead of being taken to the firing squad, Father Basil was taken into a room filled with officials. He was asked to sign a paper which stated that his death sentence was being replaced with a sentence of ten years in prison for "humanitarian reasons." Then he was transported to the concentration camps for forced labor.

He was first taken to the forested region of Kirov. Riding in the freight car was long and difficult. When they arrived it was winter and his feet were frozen. After his feet healed he was put to work clearing the forest. He remained there for almost two years.

From Kirov he was transferred to Vorkuta, beyond the Arctic Circle. In the nineteenth century when Tsar Nicholas wanted to send convicts to Vorkuta, he asked a commission to check the conditions there. The commission brought back this report: "It is too much to demand of any human being to live there."

Father Basil was in Vorkuta for most of his imprisonment, being transferred from mine to mine. Despite the exhausting work, he served the Divine Liturgy almost every day, using tins for liturgical accessories. "That tin," says Metropolitan Hermaniuk of Canada, "was his chalice, his altar, his church. Nothing was able to destroy his church, for it was based on strong conviction and God's grace." His sister Vera sent raisins which he soaked in water to make wine for the Divine Liturgy.

Life in the camps was horrendous. Once the prisoners staged a strike and when no settlement was reached, a militia surrounded the camp and opened fire. Sixty-four prisoners were killed and two hundred wounded. Father Basil was accused of causing the

Father Basil with his mother in 1957.

strike, and transferred to Vladimir, a notorious prison on the Kliazma River near Moscow.

Father Basil wrote to Moscow about his unjust sentence and the authorities transferred him back to Vorkuta. However, the directors of the mines were now afraid of him because of his unbreakable character and great spiritual strength and he was assigned to work in the camp hospital. That may have saved his life because his health was greatly deteriorated and the hospital assignment did not involve hard labor.

IN THE UNDERGROUND CHURCH

On July 9, 1955, Father Basil was released from prison. He chose to live in Lviv where he found that the Church had been completely repressed as an illegal entity. No Ukrainian Catholic Churches were open, so he became active in the underground church. He lived in a small room with a Redemptorist Brother where he would celebrate the Divine Liturgy, conduct spiritual exercises, train seminarians, and provide spiritual leadership. Being in the center of the city, the room became a meeting place

Crosses mark the spot on the floor where priests and bishops were ordained by Bishop Basil in the 1960s.

for Redemptorists and others. They shared information and encouraged one another in their ministries and Christian life. Father Basil lived here until 1969 when he was again arrested.

In 1959, Father Basil was appointed a bishop of the Ukrainian Catholic Church. Bishop Nicholas Charnetsky was already dead and there were no other Ukrainian Catholic bishops in Ukraine. The only other was Metropolitan Josyf Slipyj who was in the prison camps.

In 1963, when Metropolitan Josyf Slipyj was released after eighteen years in prison and was on his way to Rome, he sent word to Father Basil to come to Moscow to a certain hotel and meet him. Father Basil boarded the next train. When he arrived at the hotel room, Metropolitan Slipyj asked the others to leave the room. Once alone, he began the Rite of Ordination for the episcopacy. In that hotel room, Father Basil Velychkovsky was consecrated a bishop. No sooner was the service finished when the door opened and the authorities took Metropolitan Josyf to the airport for Rome. Thus Bishop Basil Velychkovsky became the only living hierarch for the Ukrainian Catholic Church in Ukraine.

Plaque marking home of Blessed Basil in Lviv from 1955–1969, after he came back from his first imprisonment.

Bishop Basil returned to Lviv and secretly began to do his episcopal work. His small room became a chancery and a cathedral. There he ordained priests and, in 1964, he consecrated a fellow Redemptorist, Father Volodymyr Sterniuk, as bishop with the right of succession. Since he was a bishop, Basil now had to be even more careful of the Soviet authorities.

HIS SECOND IMPRISONMENT

In 1968, the police undertook a massive search of the homes of Ukrainian Catholic priests. The centenary of the birth of Lenin was drawing near, and the bolshevik regime tried every possible means to mark the jubilee of their founder's birth by finally eradicating the "remnants of religion."

On October 18, the Soviets began their shake-up in Lviv, searching the homes of Ukrainian Catholic priests. Police confiscated everything religious: vestments, books and sermons, crosses, even photographic and recording equipment. They also broke into Bishop Velychkovsky's home and destroyed his prayer room.

Icon of the Mother of Perpetual Help.

On January 2, 1969, the police arrested him. Government newspapers reported his crime: anti-government activity revealed by his manuscript "The History of the Miraculous Icon of the Mother of God of Perpetual Help." Multiple copies of the book had been done on a typewriter and distributed by Father Basil. He was also charged with listening to radio broadcasts from the Vatican.

The court sentenced him to three years imprisonment with psychological torture. Bishop Basil served his sentence at Komunarsk in the Donbas region of Eastern Ukraine. After a few months there he became seriously ill and his sister sent several petitions to the government, including the Supreme Soviet, requesting her brother's release. The Soviets did not reply, but forbade him to write his sister. With no news from him for a long time, the rumor became widespread that Velychkovsky had died in prison.

Komunarsk was his most terrible imprisonment. The bishop became sick with heart disease and his feet began to swell so that he was unable to walk. At the point of death, he begged to be taken to the hospital but was refused. Then, for some reason, the administration replaced the prison director with a Ukrainian official who, having mercy on the bishop, immediately took him to the hospital.

An older woman doctor, who may have recognized him, treated him. After a week, the swelling in his feet subsided, but he never fully regained his health. The drugs administered in the prison hospital were meant to cause a heart attack so he would die. However, certain nurses pitied him and faked his injections into the mattress. Thus, he lasted longer than the authorities expected.

On January 27, 1972, Bishop Basil completed his second imprisonment. This time the Bolshevik regime did not allow him to return to Lviv. Instead, they sent him to Kiev and there issued him a departure visa to Yugoslavia. The government concealed from him his expulsion from the USSR. By then they knew he was a bishop and they did not want to have a bishop of the Ukrainian Catholic Church around. Also, his health was ruined and Moscow did not want him to die in their prison.

Father Basil recounts the terms of his expulsion:

They told me that a little rest would not hurt me and that my sister would be glad if I visited her. So I found myself on an airplane to Yugoslavia with passport in hand, and a visa "for an undetermined term" beyond the border. This was their devious method of banishing me from Ukraine.

His Final Year

After resting in Yugoslavia with his sister, the bishop journeyed to Rome, staying with His Beatitude Cardinal Josyf Slipyj. Pope Paul VI warmly received him in audience for over forty minutes. Metropolitan Maxim Hermaniuk, C.Ss.R., of Winnipeg, invited Bishop Velychkovsky to reside in Canada. He arrived there on June 15, 1972.

Bishop Basil traveled extensively throughout Canada and the United States visiting various Ukrainian Catholic eparchies, giving clergy retreats, and attending conferences and liturgical celebrations. Everywhere he spoke of the persecuted church, the importance of faith in Jesus Christ, and of committing one's life to God.

In February 1973, Bishop Basil again became seriously ill. He remained for a lengthy time in a Winnipeg hospital. His illness was clearly caused by the maltreatment and exile of the Soviets. The prison with its severe regimen completely undermined his strong constitution. Before being imprisoned, Bishop Velychkovsky was a tall man with a strong body. Afterward, his appearance changed considerably and his health was shattered.

Living his last days in Canada, Bishop Basil was quiet and subdued. But when he spoke about the Lord and the Virgin Mary his spirit came alive and shone in his voice. The strength of his Christian and national commitment is understood in his words given on June 16, 1973 in Utica, New York.

I bring you greetings from Ukraine, from your own native Church, from the Ukrainian youth, all of whom pray secretly lest the enemy see and hear. The Holy Faith maintains us. Our people live with God, and God strengthens our faithful people and nation. The Word of God passes from mouth to mouth. We are kept together by love, which reveals itself in mutual assistance, as with the first Christians. Our people share their scraps of bread which have not yet been taken away by the occupant. The Ukrainian nation is, in the faith of the forefathers, indomitable; it has not been broken by famine, tortures, prisons, exile to Siberia. The Protectress of Ukraine, the Mother of God, defends us: she lifts up her prayers before the throne of the Almighty for the Ukrainian nation.

Bishop Basil during last year of his life in Canada.

This was his last public speech for he again became seriously ill. Upon his return to Winnipeg he was hospitalized. The
slow-working drug given him in the Ukrainian prison-hospital
was finally causing his death. On Saturday, June 30, 1973, weak-
ened and wasted by years of imprisonment and suffering, the
heart of Bishop Basil Vsevolod Velychkovsky, Bishop of Lutsk,
martyr of the faith, stopped beating.

Bishop Basil did not like to talk about his prison stay, but we know he endured much suffering. Upon seeing nurses and doctors at a hospital in Winnipeg, he was overcome with such terror that he broke into cold sweats and his heart beat frightfully. The sight of medical personnel reminded him of tortures undergone in prison. Doctors reported from his autopsy that his body displayed indications of torture, including scars from electrical burns.

His funeral lasted three days. Funeral services were held July 3 in the Redemptorist Church of St. Joseph and on July 4 in the Cathedral of Ss. Volodymyr and Olha. On July 5, in the same Cathedral, the Funeral Divine Liturgy was celebrated. Ukrainian Catholic bishops from North America and Australia attended. His remains were interred in All Saints Cemetery, north of Winnipeg.

It is evident that Bishop Velychkovsky was a holy man. Even in his youth he desired to dedicate himself to the service of God. He gave himself completely to apostolic work; even in prison he was an apostle. Prison life did not break him, but strengthened his trust and commitment to God.

CHRONOLOGY OF
BLESSED BASIL VSEVOLOD VELYCHKOVSKY

June 1, 1903: Basil is born in Stanyslaviv, Western Ukraine, to Father Volodymyr and Anna. He is born into a priestly family.

1905–1911: Basil lives in Shuparets and is schooled at home.

May 1911: After a mission, Basil is dedicated and publicly consecrated to the Mother of God before her altar.

1911–1912: Studies in Probizhnia his grandfather's town.

1913–1914: Studies at the Institute of St. Josaphat in Buchach.

1914–1915: During World War I, he goes home and studies there.

1916–1917: The Velychkovsky children were evacuated to the grandfather's home in Probizhnia.

1917–1918: Basil attends high school in Horodenka.

1918: Basil joins the Ukrainian Riflemen fighting the Polish army.

1919–1920: Basil is arrested and later escapes.

1920: He enrolls in the high school in Stanyslaviv.

1921–1924: Basil studies at the Major Seminary in Lviv. In the fall of 1923 he is ordained to the diaconate.

August 2, 1924: Basil begins his novitiate for the Redemptorists in Holosko.

August 29, 1925: Basil makes his temporary profession of vows for three years.

October 9, 1925: He is ordained to the priesthood in Zboisk by Bishop Joseph Bocian, Bishop of Lutsk.

1925–1927: Father Basil teaches at the Minor Seminary in Zboisk.

1927–1928: Father Basil is transferred to Stanyslaviv to preach missions.

1928–1935: Father Basil works with Father Nicholas Charnetsky in Volyn.

1935–1939: Father Basil again does missionary work out of Stanyslaviv.

1938–1941: Father Bail is named superior of the monastery in Stanyslaviv.

1940: After conducting a religious procession on the Feast of Our Mother of Perpetual Help, he is interrogated by the NKVD.

1941: In September, he goes to Greater Ukraine, to Kamianets Podilsk to do mission work.

1942–1943: He is assigned to the monastery in Ternopil.

1943: He returns to Stanyslaviv, continuing his missionary and retreat work.

1944: Father Basil volunteers to go to the battlefront in Ternopil and stay at the Redemptorist monastery.

July 26, 1945: Father Basil is arrested in Ternopil for refusing to join the Russian Orthodox Church.

1945–1947: Father is interred and interrogated in internal KGB prison in Kiev.

Fall 1947: He is condemned to the firing squad and is placed on death row. His death sentence is commuted and he spends ten years in the Soviet gulag camps at Kirov, Vorkuta, and Vladimir.

1955: Father Basil is released from prison and returns to Lviv.

1959: He is secretly appointed as a bishop, however no one is available to consecrate him.

1963: Metropolitan Josyf Slipyj consecrates Father Basil as bishop in a hotel room in Moscow.

1964: Bishop Basil ordains Father Volodymyr Sterniuk, C.Ss.R., to the episcopacy to help him in his work in the underground Church.

January 2, 1969: Bishop Basil is arrested again, accused of anti-government activity, for his publication and dissemination of the booklet "The History of the Miraculous Icon of the Mother of God of Perpetual Help." He was sentenced for a three-year imprisonment in the severe prison at Komunarsk in the Donbas region of Ukraine.

January 27, 1972: Bishop Basil is released from prison and exiled to Yugoslavia.

June 15, 1972: Bishop Basil arrives in Winnipeg as a guest of Metropolitan Maxim Hermaniuk, C.Ss.R.

February 1973: Bishop Basil become seriously ill.

July 30, 1973: Bishop Basil dies in Winnipeg, Manitoba, Canada, and is buried in All Saints Cemetery in Winnipeg.

Chapter 3

IVAN ZIATYK, C.SS.R.
1899–1952

⸙

Ivan Ziatyk was born December 26, 1899, in Odrekhova, fifteen miles or so southwest of Sanok (now part of Poland). His parents, Stepan and Maria, were poor peasants. When Ivan was fourteen years old, his father died, leaving the child to be reared by his mother and elder brother Mykhailo.

As a child, Ivan was quiet and obedient. He was a gifted student with a profound piety. After attending secondary school at the Sanok Gymnasium, Ivan entered the Ukrainian Catholic Seminary in Peremyshl in 1919. He graduated with distinction on June 30, 1923, and was ordained a priest.

From 1925–1935 Father Ziatyk was prefect of the seminary from which he graduated. In addition to the spiritual care of the seminarians, he taught catechetics and dogmatic theology. During those years, Father Ivan also served as spiritual leader and catechist for the Ukrainian Girls' Gymnasium in Peremyshl.

JOINING THE REDEMPTORISTS

Father Ivan had great kindness and spiritual depth. He made lasting impressions on those around him. For many years he had desired to join a religious congregation. To the disdain of his local church superiors, in July 1935, Father Ivan decided to join the Redemptorists.

Much older than his fellow novices, they would often tease him as the "gray" old man. He did not seek special status in the novitiate, but accepted the duties of novices, such as washing floors, taking out garbage, and working in the garden, even though the previous year he was professor at a major seminary.

After completing his novitiate in Holosko (near Lviv) in 1936, Father Ivan was assigned to the monastery of Our Lady of Perpetual Help in Stanyslaviv (now Ivano-Frankivsk); however, he did not stay long. The next year he moved to Lviv to the monastery on Zyblikevych Street where he was the monastery's bursar and vicar.

In 1934, the Redemptorists opened a seminary in Holosko, and Father Ivan joined its faculty as professor of Scripture and dogmatic theology. From 1941 to 1944, he was assigned to the monastery of the Dormition of the Mother of God in Ternopil; and from 1944 to 1946, he was superior of the monastery of Our Lady of Perpetual Help in Zboisk (near Lviv) at the Redemptorist minor seminary.

Father Ivan was a very good leader, serene and detached from the world, and a good example for his confreres, especially in prayer. He had a gift for preaching and confessing. One would find long lines of penitents waiting to receive the sacrament of penance from him.

Ivan Ziatyk, C.Ss.R.

THE AFTERMATH OF THE WAR

The end of World War II began a terrible period in the history of Ukraine, of the Ukrainian Greek-Catholic Church, and of the Lviv Province of the Redemptorists. All Ukrainian bishops had been arrested. Early in 1946, Soviet secret police gathered Redemptorists from Ternopil, Stanyslaviv, Lviv, and Zboisk, brought them to Holosko, and placed them in an unheated wing of the monastery. Father Ivan was among them. For two years the Redemptorists were under surveillance. The men were often

87

interrogated, being promised various benefits in exchange for betraying their faith and monastic vocation. On October 17, 1948, all the Redemptorists in Holosko were transported to the Studite monastery in Univ.

Soon the Redemptorist Provincial Father Joseph De Vocht was deported to Belgium. Before departing he transferred the duties of provincial of the Lviv Province and of Vicar General of the Ukrainian Greek-Catholic Church to Father Ziatyk. Thus Father Ivan became highly suspect to the police.

In January of 1950 he was arrested. After numerous interrogations, on February 4, 1950, Father Ivan was charged in these words: "Ivan Ziatyk indeed has been a member of the Redemptorist order since 1936; he promotes the ideas of the Roman Pope of spreading the Catholic Faith among the nations of the whole world and of making all Catholics."

The investigation of Father Ziatyk's case lasted two years. He spent the entire period in Lviv and Zolochiv prisons. During the period he was interrogated seventy-two times. Interrogations often took place in the middle of the night. Witnesses claim he was often beaten very hard. Soviet authorities brought in his relatives to persuade him to sign papers betraying his faith, just so that he could be released.

One of his nephews described the following scene: Then the Soviets told me: "You will ask him to sign a paper accepting Orthodoxy and to tell us about the church." When they brought him into my presence, it was difficult to recognize him. We begged him: "Uncle, take this and sign it, and they will release you." But Father Ivan said: "No! This I will never do." Then the secret police repeated: "Sign and we will let you go with them," and my uncle responded: "May God's will be done." And then the police took him away, but despite these cruel tortures, he did not submit to the atheist regime.

IMPRISONMENT AND DEATH

In April 1951, Father Ivan was taken from Lviv to Kiev where his case was to be heard. He was kept in solitary confinement for five months. In November, he was sentenced to ten years imprisonment for "cooperating with anti-Soviet nationalistic organization and anti-Soviet propaganda." The term was served in Ozernyi Laager prison camp near the town of Bratsk in Irkutsk region.

During his imprisonment, Father Ziatyk suffered terrible torture. According to witnesses, on Good Friday 1952, Father Ivan was assigned to empty the latrine. Some of the water spilled and that gave the guard an excuse to club Father Ivan. He beat him severely. The guard then poured water on Father Ivan. It was a bitter Siberian day. The beatings and the cold caused his death in a prison hospital on May 17, 1952. Father Ivan was buried in Taishet district of Irkutsk region.

Father Ziatyk gave his life in order to not in any way deny Christ or his Church. In his union with Christ he bore his sufferings and tortures. On Good Friday, he joined Jesus on the cross. He laid down his life for the glory of God and the crown of the Church.

Chapter 4

ZYNOVIY (ZENON) KOVALYK, C.SS.R.

1903–1941

F ather Zenon was crucified like Jesus. Because of his consecration to God, he placed himself into the mouth of evil,
taking upon himself all the sufferings and pain it gave. Father
Zenon was among those spiritual warriors who run into battle,
with the truth of the Gospel as his stronghold and anchor.

Father Zenon Kovalyk was born August 18, 1903, in Ivachiv
Horishniy near Ternopil to a poor peasant family. Before becoming a Redemptorist, he worked as a primary-school teacher. He
had a strong character and never compromised his faith. The
dream of Zenon's childhood was to become a priest. Discover-
ing his vocation to the consecrated life, Zenon Kovalyk joined
the Redemptorists and professed first vows on August 28, 1926.
Shortly after this, Zenon went to Belgium for philosophy and
theology studies.

On August 9, 1932, Zenon Kovalyk was ordained a priest in
Ukraine. On September 4, he served his first Divine Liturgy in
his home village Ivachiv. The commemorative card of his ordination bore the following inscription:

O Jesus, receive me [as a sacrifice] together with the Holy Sacrifice of Your Flesh and Blood. Receive it for the Holy Church, for my Congregation and for my Motherland. Bless my parents, family, friends and all those dear to me. O Mary, my dear Mother, protect my priesthood. And you, my friends, when you see this card, pray for a moment for the one God has seen fit to become a priest, pray for him and he will remember you every day during the Divine Liturgy.

Little did Father Kovalyk know that those words were prophetic, and that soon—in just nine years—they would come true in his martyrdom.

REDEMPTORIST APOSTOLATE

After ordination, Father Kovalyk departed with Bishop Nicholas Charnetsky, C.Ss.R., to Volyn as a missionary working with the Orthodox for re-union with the Holy See of Rome. The young priest was a joy to his confreres. Father Zenon had a good sense of humor, a beautiful voice, and clear diction. He was a great singer and a truly "golden-mouthed" preacher. His apostolic zeal attracted thousands of people. Father Kovalyk loved the Mother of God with all his heart. He inflamed devotion to her among his listeners. Father Zenon had great success as a missionary.

Having spent several years working in Volyn, Father Zenon was transferred to Stanyslaviv (now Ivano-Frankivsk) to conduct missions, both in the city and in suburban villages. Immediately before the Soviet invasion of 1939, he moved to Lviv, to the Redemptorist monastery on Zyblikevych Street, and became the monastery's bursar. It was a difficult time to be a bursar because of the hardship and poverty during wartime. An added burden making it difficult to provide basic necessities for the monastery was that the NKVD set up quarters on the first floor of the monastery, confining the Redemptorists to the second

Zenon Kovalyk, C.Ss.R.

floor. One had to pass the scrutiny of the NKVD whenever one brought any supplies home.

Because of his position as bursar, he frequently visited the Metropolitan's residence to seek advice. These visits caused the Soviets to suspect him of being an agent of the Metropolitan.

While most of the Western Ukrainians were overpowered by terror, Father Zenon displayed admirable courage bringing the Word of God to people even after the Soviet invasion.

Most preachers were extremely cautious, trying to avoid burning issues of the day and merely exhorting people to be faithful to God. Father Kovalyk, on the contrary, openly condemned atheistic practices of the Soviets. His sermons had great impact.

Church of the Immaculate Conception and interior where Blessed Zenon Kovalyk was preaching the day before he was arrested by the Soviets.

It was known that spies were present and would bring anti-soviet sentiments to the authorities. Much in Father Zenon's sermons could be interpreted as anti-Soviet, for he preached against the dangers of the atheistic and immoral regime.

When he was advised by friends of the danger resulting from such preaching, Father Kovalyk answered: "I will receive death gladly if such be God's will, but I shall never compromise my conscience as a preacher."

His last mission sermon took place in Ternopil on August 28, 1940, on the feast of the Dormition of the Mother of God. Father Kovalyk preached before ten thousand faithful. On that day they held a solemn procession through the city with the consecration and erection of the mission cross. This provoked the Soviet wrath.

Prison in Lviv where Blessed Zenon was crucified.

MARTYRDOM

Father Zenon's dream of martyrdom came true in just a few months. On December 20, 1940, agents of the secret police entered the Redemptorist monastery to arrest Father Kovalyk for his sermons during the novena of the Immaculate Conception of the Mother of God in the monastery's church. During the night, NKVD agents entered the monastery and demanded the list of confreres who were living there. When they came upon Father Zenon's name, they went to his room and interrogated him. Under the pretense that they needed to question him more at the station for possible passport fraud, they took him away. Everyone knew he was being arrested and would not be back soon. Before leaving, Father Zenon asked his superior for his last blessing and absolution.

Although the Redemptorists tried to find out about their confrere, it was only in April 1941 that they learned he was in

Plaque on wall of wartime prison where hundreds were killed in June of 1941, including Blessed Zenon.

prison on Zamarstynivska Street (the so-called "Brygidky" prison). During the six months of his imprisonment, Father Kovalyk underwent twenty-eight painful interrogations. After one interrogation, accompanied by especially cruel tortures, Father Kovalyk fell seriously ill due to considerable loss of blood.

wow

While in prison, Father Kovalyk continued his apostolic work. He shared a tiny (fourteen foot by twelve foot) unfurnished cell with thirty-two others. With the prisoners he prayed a third of the rosary on weekdays and the whole rosary on Sundays. Father Kovalyk also conducted liturgical prayers, prayer services to the Mother of God, and on Epiphany he treated the inmates to the liturgical consecration of water. Aside from these prayers, Father Kovalyk heard confessions, conducted spiritual exercises and catechism classes, and consoled the inmates by telling—in his peculiar humorous manner—various religious stories. No wonder that the prisoners—people in the greatest need of hope and consolation—truly loved Father Kovalyk.

In June 1941, when German troops started their offensive, the prison keepers, eager to flee but unable to take the prisoners along, started shooting the inmates. But it was not enough for them just to shoot Father Kovalyk. Reminding him of the crucified Christ, they nailed Father Kovalyk to the prison wall in the view of his fellow prisoners.

When German troops entered Lviv, they immediately opened the prisons to clean up the piles of decaying corpses. People rushed to the prisons hoping to find their relatives. As the witnesses relate, the most horrible sight was that of a priest crucified upon the prison wall, his abdomen cut open and a dead human fetus pushed into the wound.

Appendix 1

ℒIST OF MARTYRS

BISHOPS

1. *Bishop Mykolay (Nicholas) Charnetsky, C.Ss.R.*
   Blessed Nicholas Charnetsky was born on September 14, 1884. He was ordained a priest in 1909 and became a Redemptorist in 1919. In 1931, he was ordained a bishop. Arrested in April of 1945, Bishop Charnetsky spent eleven years in Soviet prison camps. He died in Lviv in 1959.

2. *Bishop Hryhori (Gregory) Khomyshyn*
   Blessed Gregory Khomyshyn was born on March 25, 1867, in the village of Hadynkivtsi, in the district of Ternopil. He was ordained a priest on November 18, 1893. Father Gregory was ordained a bishop for Stanyslaviv in 1904. In 1939, he was arrested for the first time by the NKVD (KGB) and released. His second arrest was in April 1945, and he was deported to Kiev. He died after torturous interrogations in Kiev's NKVD prison on December 28, 1945.

3. *Bishop Josaphat Kotsylovsky, O.S.B.M.*
Blessed Josaphat Kotsylovsky was born on March 3, 1876, in the village of Pakoshivka, in the region of Lemkiv. He was ordained to the priesthood on October 9, 1907. On October 2, 1911, he entered the novitiate of the Basilian Order. He was ordained to the episcopacy on September 23, 1917, in Peremyshl. In September 1945, the Polish authorities imprisoned him. He died a martyr for the faith on November 17, 1947, in a Kiev prison.

Communists?

4. *Bishop Simeon Lukach*
Blessed Simeon Lukach was born on July 7, 1893, in the village of Starunia, in the region of Stanyslaviv. In 1919 he was ordained a priest by Bishop Gregory Khomyshyn. In April 1945, it was suspected that Bishop Gregory had secretly ordained him a bishop. On October 26, 1949, he was arrested, but after numerous interrogations the KGB could not find a charge so he was finally set free on February 11, 1955. In July 1962, he was arrested once again. While in prison, Simeon was stricken with tuberculosis, and he died on August 22, 1964.

5. *Bishop Vasyl (Basil) Vsevolod Velychkovsky, C.Ss.R.*
Blessed Basil Velychkovsky was born in 1903. In 1924, he entered the Redemptorist Congregation. After being ordained a priest in 1925, Basil served as a missionary in Halychyna and Volyn. He was arrested in 1945 and sentenced to die by a firing squad. After the sentence was commuted, he spent ten years in Soviet prisons before secretly being ordained a bishop in 1963. He was arrested again in 1969 and exiled to North America in 1972. He died in Winnipeg, Manitoba, Canada, in 1973.

6. *Bishop Ivan Sleziuk*

Blessed Ivan Sleziuk was born on January 14, 1896, in the village of Zhyvachiv, Ivano-Frankivsk District. In 1923 he was ordained to the priesthood. In April 1945, Bishop Gregory Khomyshyn ordained him as his co-adjutor with right of succession. On June 2, 1945, Bishop Ivan was arrested and deported for ten years to the labor camps in Vorkuta, Russia. After his release on November 15, 1954, he returned to Ivano-Frankivsk. In 1962, he was arrested again and imprisoned for five years in a camp of strict regimen. After his release on November 30, 1968, he had to often go to the KGB for regular "talks." The last visit took place two weeks before his death, which occurred December 2, 1973, in Ivano-Frankivsk.

7. *Bishop Nicetas Budka*

Blessed Nicetas Budka was born on June 7, 1877, in the village of Dobromirka, in the district of Zbarazh. In 1905, he was ordained to the priesthood. He was consecrated bishop in Lviv on October 14, 1912. That same year he was appointed by the Holy See as the Bishop for Ukrainian Catholics in Canada. In 1928, he became vicar general of the Metropolitan Curia in Lviv. On April 11, 1945, the Soviet government imprisoned him with a sentence of eight years. He died in prison on October 1, 1949. His remains became the food for wolves.

8. *Bishop Hryhori (Gregory) Lakota*

Blessed Gregory Lakota was born on January 31, 1883, in the village of Holodivka, in the region of Lemko. He was ordained to the priesthood in 1908 in the city of Peremyshl. On May 16, 1926, he was ordained to the episcopacy and was appointed auxiliary bishop of Peremyshl. On June 9, 1946, he was arrested and imprisoned for ten years in Vorkuta, Russia. He died as a martyr for the faith on November 12, 1950, in the village of Abez, near Vorkuta.

PRIESTS

9. *Reverend Leonid Feodorov*

   Blessed Leonid Feodorov was born to a Russian Orthodox family on November 4, 1879, in St. Petersburg, Russia. In 1902 he left his Orthodox seminary and traveled to Rome, where he became Catholic. On March 25, 1911, he was ordained to the priesthood in the Eastern rite in Bosnia. There, in 1913, he became a Studite. Afterwards, he returned to St. Petersburg and was subsequently arrested and sent to Siberia. In 1917, he was released and appointed to be the head of the Russian Catholic Church of the Eastern rite, with the title of Exarch. His second arrest came in 1923, and he was sent to prison. He died as a martyr for the faith on March 7, 1935.

10. *Reverend Mykola (Nicholas) Conrad*

    Blessed Nicholas Conrad was born on May 16, 1876, in the village of Strusiv, in the district of Ternopil. In 1889, he was ordained to the priesthood. While a parish priest in the village of Stradch, near Yakiv, on June 26, 1941, he went to visit sick parishioners with the holy Eucharist despite great danger. On his way, he was abducted by bolsheviks and shot, dying a martyr's death.

11. *Reverend Andriy (Andrew) Ishchak*

    Blessed Andrew Ishchak was born on September 23, 1887, in Mykolayiv, in the district of Lviv. He was ordained in 1914. On June 26, 1941, he was caught by the Soviet army while serving at the village of Sykhiv and was executed.

12. *Reverend Roman Lysko*
Blessed Roman Lysko was born on August 14, 1914, in Heraldic, Lviv District. After marrying, he was ordained to the priesthood on August 28, 1941. On September 9, 1949, he was arrested by the NKVD and put into a prison in Lviv. He died in prison on October 14, 1949. Some accounts say he was sealed into a wall and left there to die.

13. *Reverend Mykola (Nicholas) Tsehelsky*
Blessed Nicholas Tsehelsky was born on December 17, 1896, in the village of Strusiv, district of Ternopil. After Nicholas was married, the archbishop ordained him to the priesthood on April 5, 1925. On October 28, 1946, he was arrested. On January 27, 1947, he was sentenced to ten years in prison and was deported to labor camps in Mordovia. He died on May 25, 1951, as a martyr for the faith. He is buried in the camp cemetery.

14. *Reverend Petro (Peter) Verhun*
Blessed Peter Verhun was born on November 18, 1890, in Heraldic, Lviv District. On October 30, 1927, he was ordained to the priesthood, and was appointed to be the priest for Ukrainian Catholics in Berlin, Germany. Later he became the Apostolic Visitator to Germany. In June 1945, he was arrested and sent to prison camps in Siberia. He died as a martyr for the faith on February 7, 1957, in the village of Angarskiy, in the territory of Krasnoiarsk, Russia.

15. *Reverend Oleksiy Zarytskyi*

    Blessed Oleksiy Zarytskyi was born in 1912 in the village of Biche, in the region of Lviv. He was ordained to the priesthood in 1936. In 1948, he was imprisoned for ten years. Shortly after his early release in 1957, he was imprisoned again for a three-year term. He died as a martyr for the faith on October 30, 1963, in a labor camp in a village near Karaganda.

16. *Reverend Archmandrite Clement Sheptytsky*

    Blessed Clement Sheptytsky was born on November 17, 1869, in the village of Prylbychi, in the district of Lviv. In 1911 he entered the Studites. On August 28, 1915, he was ordained to the priesthood. On June 5, 1947, he was arrested by NKVD and sentenced to eight years of hard labor. He died as a martyr for the faith on May 1, 1951, in the Vladimir prison.

17. *Reverend Severian Baranyk, O.S.B.M.*

    Blessed Severian Baranyk was born on July 18, 1889. On September 24, 1904, he entered the Basilian Order and made his final vows on September 21, 1910. He was ordained to the priesthood on February 14, 1915. On June 26, 1941, the NKVD arrested him, after which he was never seen alive again; however, a boy later give witness to seeing the tortured and swollen corpse of Father Severian, marked with a cross-shaped knife slash on his chest.

18. *Reverend Yakym (Joachim) Senkivskyi, O.S.B.M.*

    Blessed Joachim Senkivskyi was born on May 2, 1896, in the village of Hayi Velykyi, in the district of Ternopil. He was ordained a priest on December 4, 1921. In 1923, he became a novice in the Basilian

Order in Krekhiv. In 1939, he was appointed to be superior at the monastery in Drohobych. On June 26, 1941, he was arrested by the Communists and on June 29 was martyred by being boiled to death in a cauldron in the Drohobych prison.

19. *Reverend Zenoviy (Zenon) Kovalyk, C.Ss.R.*
    Blessed Zenon Kovalyk was born on August 18, 1903, in the village of Ivachiv in the district of Ternopil. He was professed as a Redemptorist on August 28, 1926, and ordained a priest on September 4, 1932. Arrested on December 20, 1940, he was martyred by crucifixion at the end of June 1941.

20. *Reverend Vitaliy Bayrak, O.S.B.M.*
    Blessed Vitaliy Bayrak was born on February 24, 1907, in the village of Shvaikivtsy, in the district of Ternopil. On September 4, 1924, he entered the Basilian Order and was ordained a priest on August 13, 1933. On September 17, 1945, the NKVD arrested Father Vitaliy and he was sentenced to eight years in a labor camp. Just prior to Easter of 1946, Father Vitaliy died after having been severely beaten in the Drohobych prison.

21. *Reverend Ivan Ziatyk, C.Ss.R.*
    Blessed Ivan Ziatyk was born on December 26, 1899, in the village of Odrekhova near Sanok. In 1923 he was ordained to the priesthood. In 1935 he joined the Redemptorists. On January 5, 1950, he was arrested and sent away to a prison in Ozernyi, Russia. On Good Friday in 1952 he was severely tortured by clubbing and died on May 17.

Religious Women and Laity

22. *Sister Laurentia Herasymiv, S.S.J.*

Blessed Laurentia Herasymiv was born on September 31, 1911, in the village of Rudnyky, in the district of Lviv. In 1931 she entered the Sisters of St. Joseph, and in 1933 made her first vows. In the Spring of 1950, she was arrested by the agents of the NKVD and sent to Borislav. Thereafter, she was exiled to Tomsk in Siberia. On June 30, 1950, she was relocated to the village of Kharsk. She continued to pray frequently and did much demanding manual labor. She patiently endured subhuman conditions. She died on August 28, 1952, in the village of Kharsk in the Tomsk Region of Siberia.

23. *Sister Tarsykia Matskiv, S.S.M.I.*

Blessed Tarsykia Matskiv was born on March 23, 1919, in the village of Khodoriv, Lviv District. On May 3, 1938, she entered the Sister Servants of Mary Immaculate. After professing her first vows on November 5, 1940, she worked in her convent. Even prior to the arrival of the bolsheviks in Lviv, Sister Tarsykia made a private oath to her spiritual director, Father Volodymyr Kovalyk, O.S.B.M., that she would sacrifice her life for the conversion of Russia and for the good of the Catholic Church. The bolsheviks were determined to destroy the convent. On the morning of July 18, 1944, at 8:00 A.M., a Soviet soldier rang the convent door. When Sister Tarsykia answered the door she was shot without warning, and died.

24. *Sister Olympia Bida, S.S.J.*

    Blessed Olympia Bida was born in 1903 in the village of Tsebliv, Lviv District. She entered the Sisters of St. Joseph and served in various towns and villages as a catechist, director of novices, and attendant to the aged and infirm. She was appointed superior of the convent in the town of Kheriv. In 1950 she was arrested with two other sisters, and exiled to the Tomsk region of Siberia. Succumbing to a serious illness, she died on January 28, 1952.

25. *Volodymyr Pryjma*

    Blessed Volodymyr Pryjma was born on July 17, 1906, in the village of Stradch, Yavoriv District. After graduating from a school for cantors, he became the cantor and choir director in the village church of Stradch. On June 26, 1941, agents of the NKVD mercilessly tortured and murdered him along with Father Nicholas Conrad in the forest near their village as they were returning from the home of a sick woman who had requested the sacrament of penance.

ℛAYERS TO THE UKRAINIAN CATHOLIC MARTYRS

EASTERN CHURCH PRAYERS FOR THE MARTYRS

TROPAR

O Passion-bearers of the Lord!
O you who bore the Lord's suffering!
Blessed is the earth that drank your blood.
And the holy temples that received your bodies.
For you conquered the enemy on the day of
    judgment
And boldly proclaimed Christ.
Pray to him, as the Good One, to save us.

KONDAK

O divine Martyrs,
You have become great lights
Enlightening all creation with your work.
You heal the sick and disperse the profound darkness.
Pray unceasingly to Christ our God for us all.

PRAYERS FROM VESPERS OF THE MARTYRS

O great and glorious Martyrs,
Through your wisdom you have humbled the
    enemy
Who tried by force to lead you from God.
Having suffered patiently and righteously,
You wove for yourselves a crown of victory
And now you are praying for us.

EXULATION

We extol you, O holy Martyrs,
And we honor your sufferings, which you endured
for Christ.

V: God is our protection and our strength,
     He is our help in time of trouble.

V: They spilled their blood as if it were water

V: The memory of the just will be forever,
     Of evil hearsay they will not fear.

PRAYER TO OUR REDEMPTORIST MARTYRS

O Lord, our God,
You have so loved us,
that You sent your Son Jesus
who showed us the way of perfection
through the way of the Cross.

He was obedient to You, His Father,
and took the form of a servant,
even unto death,
Therefore, You have exalted Him
and given the name Lord.

You call all to believe in You
and to follow Your way.
We thank You for the grace
you gave to Nicholas Charnetsky,
Basil Velychkovsky, Ivan Ziatyk, and
    Zenon Kovalyk
and to all the other spiritual companions,
such that they were able to pay
the ultimate price of faithfulness to You
in giving their lives.
Their love for You
caused them to die,
so as not to betray You and Your Truth.

We thank you for glorifying them
in your heavenly kingdom,
that they may be for all of us
a shining example of Your powerful presence
    in our lives.
That which is impossible for us
is possible through You, our Lord and Master.

We pray that You give us
the grace of faithfulness
    and generosity
as we seek to respond to Your love.
Through their intercession,
help us to always stand firm in the Truth
and be faithful to You and Your commandments.
Through their intercession,
we humbly ask You for this particular favor
    (ask for particular favor here).

For all the glory and honor belongs to You,
Almighty Father, Eternal Son and Life-giving
    Spirit,
now and for ever and ever.

O Holy Mother of God and our Mother of
    Perpetual Help,
whom our Redemptorist Martyrs loved so dearly,
lead us to Your Son Jesus.
Give us the courage always to follow Him
in all the circumstances of our life.
We place ourselves under your protection.
Amen.